ETERNITY

Fr Ken Barker MGL

Connor Court Publishing

Connor Court Publishing Pty Ltd

Copyright © Ken Barker MGL, 2022

ALL RIGHTS RESERVED. This book contains material protected under International and Federal Copyright Laws and Treaties. Any unauthorised reprint or use of this material is prohibited. No part of this book may be reproduced or transmitted in any form or by any means, electronic or mechanical, including photocopying, recording, or by any information storage and retrieval system without express written permission from the publisher.

PO Box 7257
Redland Bay QLD 4165
sales@connorcourt.com
www.connorcourt.com

ISBN: 9781923224780

Cover design by Lawrence Yuen MGL

Printed in Australia

CONTENTS

	FOREWORD	vii
	INTRODUCTION	1
1	MYSTERY OF DEATH	17
2	JUDGEMENT	35
3	COMMUNION OF SAINTS	47
4	HEAVEN	57
5	PURGATORY	71
6	HELL	79
7	RESURRECTION OF THE BODY	99
8	SECOND COMING	111
9	NEW HEAVEN AND NEW EARTH	127
10	LET US PROCLAIM THE GOOD NEWS	133
	ENDNOTES	145
	APPENDIX	151

Acknowledgements and Dedication

I wish to thank Selina Hasham for her careful examination of the text, and Lawrence Yuen MGL for the cover design. Also I am grateful to the MGL brothers who are my source of inspiration and encouragement.

    I dedicate this book to my beloved Mother Phyllis who peacefully entered eternal life on 2 October 2014, and in memory of my brother Ross who recently died. I also remember with gratitude those MGL brothers who also have gone to the Lord – Fr Dean Braun, Br Paul Nixon, Br Mark O'Dea, and Br Albert Pastera. May they all be wrapped in the love of God forever.

FOREWORD

To write about eternity is a great challenge for anyone. Theologians and philosophers have pondered the meaning for centuries.

However, our Catholic faith tells us that eternal life is a unique gift from God, foreshadowed and fulfilled by the Resurrection of Jesus.

It is not an inherent part of human existence but a unique moment through which death is conquered once for all, permitting Christians to know and experience eternal life.

Although physical death still happens, those who believe in Christ and live good lives will experience eternal life in Heaven.

Contrasted with mortal life, eternal existence is the timeless state into which the soul passes at a person's death.

Our faith also tells us that an unrepentant sinner is someone who does not regret the things they have done wrong and refuses God's offer of forgiveness and salvation through Jesus.

Thinking about eternity is not however something which preoccupies the thoughts of most people. The immediate seems more important and decidedly more comfortable.

Fr Barker, in his Introduction, tells the story of Arthur Stace, an alcoholic on the streets of Sydney, who underwent an extraordinary transformation when he heard a preaching at St Barnabas Church Broadway. He became convinced of the importance of eternity. For 30 years he surreptitiously wrote the word "Eternity" on Sydney pavements. When his identity was finally discovered he simply explained, "I hope I am helping people to know that there is an Eternity to face and to be living for it is a lovely thing to know!"

While discussions on eternity are often passionate and lively, Arthur's words are simple, clear, and heartfelt.

When applied to God, the term "Eternity " does not mean a long, long time. It means God is outside of time altogether.

Over many years and numerous words, philosophers have spoken of three different views of eternity.

There is the view that says only the present is real; the view that says only the past and present are real and the view that the past, present, and future are all real.

And then there is the argument from physics. Albert Einstein proposed that time is essentially another dimension, a fourth dimension alongside the three spatial dimensions we experience: height, width, and breadth. Einstein proposed that, together, these dimensions make up a reality physicists have called "spacetime". This has made it easier to describe physical phenomena using equations – proving very useful to scientists.

So the debate about the nature of time has been going on for a very long time.

Although the Church does not have an official teaching on the nature of time, what the Church does teach about God has implications for the nature of time. The *Catechism of the Catholic Church* states: "We firmly believe and confess without reservation that there is only one true God, eternal, infinite (immensus), and unchangeable, incomprehensible, almighty and ineffable, the

Father the Son and the Holy Spirit; three persons indeed, but one essence, substance or nature entirely simple (*CCC*, 202).

The classic theological explanation of eternity was provided in the sixth century by the Roman philosopher Boethius. He wrote, "Eternity ... is the simultaneously whole and perfect possession of interminable life" (*On the Consolation of Philosophy*, 5:6). This means that God's life has no end (it is interminable), and that He possesses all of that life all at once (in a simultaneously whole manner). He does not experience it moment by moment the way we do. God's, life is therefore, not spread out over time.

Closer to our worldly time Saint John Paul II wrote, "His Eternity ... must be understood as the 'indivisible perfect, and simultaneous possession of an unending life,'' and therefore as the attribute of being absolutely "beyond time" (John Paul II, Audience, 4 September 1985).

It is only natural to ask what will eternity be like? How might we have spoken of life after death to a man who simply took up his chalk when he found the peace of Christ?

Perhaps I would have said that I believe we will be enveloped in the glorious love of God and the Communion of Saints, rejoicing forever and experiencing the love, glory, wisdom and beauty of God perfected and deepened. We will be complete and lacking in nothing. Until then we continue on a pilgrim's journey.

I believe the words of Fr Ken Barker in this book will be a wonderful guide for you on your journey.

Most Rev Anthony Randazzo
Bishop of Broken Bay

INTRODUCTION

In a reverie, I find myself gazing upon the bustling crowds in one of our modern cities. I feel in my heart a deep compassion for each person. It seems like I am with Jesus when he looked out upon the crowds and felt wrenched in the guts "because they were harassed and dejected, like sheep without a shepherd" (Mt 9:36). God's grace is working on my hardened heart; I am moved deeply, touched by the merciful heart of Jesus. The compassion rising in my heart is not through any merit of my own, but simply a gift from on high. I sense the heart of Jesus; opened radically for every man, woman and child on the face of the earth. He has come to save all. As I reflect upon the crowd, I do not see a *'massa damnata'* destined for the fires of hell. Nevertheless, I am moved deeply that so many are lost without a clear purpose in life, heavily burdened and confused by the vagaries of life, and with no answer to the gnawing meaninglessness of modern living. I sense the heart of Jesus for the 'lost'. In his name I want to bring his invitation to each person in the crowd, "Come to me all you who labour and are heavy burdened and I will give you rest. Take up my yoke and learn from me, for I am gentle and humble of heart, and you will have rest for your souls. For my yoke is easy and my burden light" (Mt11:28-30). An invitation to find true peace in the heart of Jesus, which can be found nowhere else. There is no condemnation in the heart of Jesus (Rom 8:1). His whole being radiates mercy; that no one would be lost in this earthly sojourn, and, even more, that no one be lost eternally.

Unfortunately, the Church is perceived by many of our contemporaries as judging harshly and condemning all those who put 'none' on their census in regard to religion, or those who have wandered away from the Church due to scandal or numerous other reasons. Maybe there is truth here; at least our language can sometimes appear to place ourselves in a superior position before others since we are the 'enlightened' ones. Jesus himself spent much energy rebuking that sort of pharisaic attitude. But when the Church is truly herself she will be like a mother welcoming in respectful dialogue and acceptance, and offering a place of comfort and healing for those who are mysteriously drawn by the grace of God.

Christ is the light beckoning all to come to him; those in the darkness of despair, those who have lost their way and can see no sure path, those who have courted worldly glory but have become unstuck, those who have found themselves in the grip of addiction with seemingly no way out, those who are blind because of inherent arrogance and pride. I can sense the precariousness of the lives of so many. Not that God has anyone marked out for failure, disgrace or condemnation. Yet without Christ they cannot find their true path to life. His anguished heart shows the depth of his love for each person. This was the eternal love that took him to Calvary; the love of his wounded heart pierced for our sake. On the cross he held each one of these millions of people in his heart. He did not die just for the collective, but for each individual, and this is the revelation that every human person desperately needs. Without knowing Jesus as the way, people will wander adrift, like a ship without its mooring, like a sheep lost in a desert, like a miner in the darkness of a collapsed cave.

We Christians feel impelled to offer the good news of the saving love of God in Jesus Christ. We know what joy comes to the human heart when people open themselves to an encounter with the risen Lord! Nothing else can minister this divine love that the human heart longs for most. The aching hole in the human heart, which is infinitely deep, cannot be filled by facile substitutes – pleasures, power, status, money, or whatever we desperately seek to fill the hole. Only the love of God revealed in Jesus will heal the wounded human condition. That is why I have written this book. Previously I wrote on *Amazing Love*,[1] in an attempt to describe the beautiful gift of the redemption won for us in Jesus. My focus was on the power and victory that Christ offers to us here and now. In this new book I hope to put everything in an eternal perspective. What happens now has implications for eternity!

Questions about death, heaven, purgatory, hell, judgement, and the second coming are not often dealt with in the modern era. It is as if the modern mind has closed in upon itself. Even in the Church we are to some degree complicit with this silence in regard to the 'last things'. Yet surely to be able to take the right path in this world we need to know where we are heading! But often our fumbling efforts to call people to greater awareness of things yet to come go unheeded. Sometimes they can even be comical. Once, in my early years of enthusiasm for God, when I was with the MGL brothers preaching on the streets of Canberra, I was as usual proclaiming the love of God. In a voice that was not threatening, but loud enough to hear, I was asking of passers-by "Where are you going?" I was hoping to stir up thought about the direction of life and ultimately about what happens after death. But a woman passing by in all innocence, without malice, turned to me and very sweetly answered, "My dear, I am going to Woolworths!" We all cracked up at that stage. It was an hilarious moment. I probably deserved that response. Yet maybe this story indicates how little we are accustomed to pondering on the weightier matters of death and life after death.

I shudder a little as I take up this task of writing about our eternal destiny, since of all spiritual matters this is possibly the most obscure. I remember when I wrote my first spiritual book I asked my Spiritual Director whether he thought it was a venture inspired by God. He gave me the green light, but put three conditions, a) that I be detached from whether or not it is published, b) that I gain the approval for publication from the official Church (to ensure it will be without error and c) that I only write from what I have first-hand experience. In this case, the first two conditions can be fulfilled, but not the third! No one has come back from death to tell us about it all. It is this speculative dimension that worries me. However, the saving feature will be to follow the teaching of the Church. The rest I leave in the hands of God.

Eternity

The thoughts of a modern person are not likely to turn spontaneously to eternity. We spend most of our time preoccupied with the immediate needs of the present, rarely lifting our gaze to the reality of what awaits us after death. Many would even deny the eternal. After all, to the contemporary mind, anything beyond the scrutiny of science must be questionable. No one has returned to share about it. Even those whose religious beliefs accept the credibility of eternity rarely reflect on what happens when this earthly journey finishes. It's a little too uncomfortable to ponder what happens after death; better to push it aside and get on with making the most of the time we have now.

This is why it was amazing to have the word 'Eternity' emblazoned on the iconic Sydney Harbour Bridge for the New Year celebrations ushering in the new millennium. Relatively few people would have known at that time the history behind this unlikely choice. The story began early last century with a petty criminal named Arthur Stace.[2] He made a mediocre living as a 'cockatoo' in Minnies brothel in Surry Hills, and also by acting as a scout for gambling pools warning when police were near. He was steeped in the underworld, often used by gangs of thieves and robbers as a look-out. Years later he would confess how at that time he had a 'vicious spirit'.[3]

During the First World War, Arthur took the opportunity to enlist in the Army in 1916. Having a slight physique and mediocre health he was used as a stretcher bearer in the 16th Battalion in France. However, after being impacted by an explosion he suffered severe bronchitis and pleurisy. After long hospitalisation he returned home with an honourable discharge. On arrival in Sydney there was no job or practical help. He was back on the streets. He didn't return to his petty criminal connections, but through the 1920s he was one of the many homeless drunks living out a pathetic existence on the Sydney streets with little hope, and desperate for something more to life. Years later he said he spent more time lying in the gutter than out of it.[4] He would even present himself totally drunk to the Darlinghurst police station and beg for a cell, only to be turned away.

All this changed when on 6 August 1930 Arthur walked into St Barnabas Church on Broadway to pick up a rock cake and a cuppa, which was offered free, as long as the patrons were prepared to listen to the preaching first. The preacher had a compelling message that captured Arthur. "If any of you men are sick of the lives you are living, there is One who loves you who will set you free and his name is Jesus". Arthur recalled later that during the preaching he "came under the strong conviction of sin" and desired "to be delivered from its bondage". He said he also "realised that Christ was stronger than drink". After downing his tea and eating his rock cake, he left the hall alone, crossed Broadway, and entered Victoria Park (adjacent to Sydney University). There under a large Moreton Bay fig tree he knelt down and wept. He cried out a simple prayer: "God, be merciful to me a sinner", just like the tax collector at the back of the temple in the parable told by Jesus (Lk 18:9-14). Arthur recalls, "God really met me that night in the park! ... The desire to drink was taken away! I was a changed man!"[5] Over the next 30 years whenever he had the opportunity to witness he would testify: "I went into the meeting for a rock cake and came out with the Rock of all Ages". Arthur had discovered the peace of Christ.

Arthur had an extraordinary transformation in life, giving up the grog, forsaking smoking and gambling, and refraining from swearing and blaspheming. He attributed his new freedom totally to Christ. He became active in the ministry of rehabilitating alcoholics. But there was another mission the Lord had for Arthur. In November 1932 the evangelist John Ridley was holding an Evening Service at the City Tabernacle in Darlinghurst. A large crowd of 450 people turned up on the first night, and amongst them was Arthur. Ridley preached for an hour or so. Arthur listened spellbound. The topic was "Echoes of Eternity". The preacher assured his congregation there was no other subject more momentous than eternity. Ridley proclaimed the simple truth that eternity was the life to come, the endless future after physical death. He challenged his listeners not to ignore this reality. Eternity for each one of us is determined by God - either sublime or terrible. "You have got to face it; you have got to face it" he thundered. He emphasised that even though life may be conflict ridden and full of suffering we have a blissful eternity awaiting if we turn to God. With powerful realism Ridley declared, "Death is the doorway to eternity and you must die. Yes, it is an individual journey. You must die". He insisted the most important thing you can do in life is to turn to Jesus as your Saviour and Lord. Ridley's final plea struck Arthur to the core:

> Eternity! Eternity! I wish that I could sound, or shout, that word to everyone on the streets of Sydney. Eternity! Friends, you have got to meet it. Where will you spend Eternity?

Arthur left the Church inspired. In his own words, this is what happened next:

> Eternity went ringing through my brain and suddenly I began crying and felt a powerful call from the Lord to

write 'Eternity'. I had a piece of chalk in my pocket and, outside the church, I bent down right there and wrote it.[6]

Arthur was astonished to find that he wrote the word on the pavement in perfect copperplate lettering. He saw this as a miracle. His schooling had been minimal. He said later, "I couldn't have spelt eternity for a hundred quid". Not only did he spell the word correctly he also wrote in stylish lettering that had not been learnt naturally. It was clearly a providential sign and an indication to Arthur of a mission given from God. He said, "That was the moment that decided me to start writing "Eternity" on the footpaths and I've been doing it ever since".[7]

So began a one-man hidden mission which lasted for years. He would rise early at 4am and pray for an hour. Then have a light breakfast and take public transport to the suburb chosen that day. He would spend a few hours chalking his message on the streets, writing this one-word sermon in prominent places. In one session he may write the word up to 50 times. He was a pavement evangelist. Whether it was the inner-city area, subway entrances, bus stations, schools, churches, galleries, parks, steps to courthouses, beach walkways, the message was the same and the writing identical. Without people knowing his identity Arthur soon became famous as "Mr Eternity".

From 14 November 1932, when Arthur first chalked Eternity on the pavement outside the church, until 1952 no one knew the identity of Mr Eternity, even though thousands of Sydney-siders had witnessed his message. Then one day during an inner-city outreach conducted by Arthur's church his pastor Lisle Thomas caught him in the act. "You're Mr Eternity!" he exclaimed. "Guilty, your honour!" replied Arthur, but he would not let him disclose it. So, it remained a secret, but more and more sightings led to the press beginning to take interest. The story became more and more intriguing. Then in 1955, after a few years of hesitation, Arthur allowed a booklet on his life to be published, called *The Crooked Made Straight*. It was a testimony of his conversion and a call to repentance and faith. The tract identified Arthur as "Mr Eternity". However, while the press kept speculating on the identity of Mr Eternity, the tract had not yet come into their hands.

Lisle Thompson begged Arthur to let him send the tract to the press to clear up all the false speculation. Finally he agreed. On 24 June 1956 the *Sunday Telegraph* broke the news, with the heading "The Man that Sydney's Wondered About ... Every Dawn He Chalks a Pavement Challenge". Arthur was now uncomfortably in the limelight. He was in his early 70s and slowing down. He never sought the popular attention, but he had become the author of a legend. On a 2GB interview he was asked why he spent most of his life chalking Eternity. Arthur cut straight to the point, "I believe that we're in the world for either of two things: to be a help or a hindrance. I hope I am helping people to know that there is an eternity to face and to be living for it is a lovely thing to know!"[8]

Arthur Stace died on 30 July 1967. A front page article in the *Sydney Morning Herald* had the headline, "Mr Eternity has written his last word".[9] Ten years later, just after John Ridley's death a memorial was unveiled in Sydney Square between St Andrew's Cathedral and Town Hall. Embossed in aluminium and embedded into the pavement adjacent to the waterfall you can find the word

Eternity in the same copperplate script as Arthur had scrawled in chalk on the pavements of Sydney. The architect in charge of the Sydney Square development, Ridley Smith, had been named after the famous pastor. Unveiling the memorial Smith remarked that he did so "with the hope that all of us here will be able to say, 'Meet you in eternity', while this spot may become more and more popular, causing people to say, 'Meet you at eternity'".

We are but pilgrims

Inscribed on the tomb of St Mary of the Cross MacKillop in North Sydney, are her words, "Remember we are but travellers here". We are but pilgrims on this earthly journey. Our true homeland is in heaven. There is our lasting meeting place. As pilgrims we have no ultimate resting place here. We need to keep an eternal perspective. Otherwise, we will mistake some earthly reality as the source of ultimate joy. Everything we experience here on this earthly journey, all that is so good, true and beautiful, should not mesmerise us, deluding us to think this is all we are made for. Rather it should point us towards the ultimate Goodness, Truth and Beauty. The psalmist tells us, "In God alone is my soul at rest … He alone is my rock, my stronghold, my fortress" (Ps 62:1-2). My ultimate joy is found in God alone. As the well-known saying of St Augustine, "You have made us for yourself, O God, and our hearts are restless until they rest in you."[10] Those of us who grew up with the old green Catechism know how it defined our purpose in being created: "to serve God here on earth and to be with him forever in heaven". In current popular sentiment within the Church the first part of that definition is applauded, but the second part is largely forgotten, or unconsciously suppressed. We are meant ultimately for heaven, and the way we live in this earthly sojourn will determine whether we fulfill this purpose.

Years ago, when I read the life-story of Thomas Merton, a famous American Trappist monk, I was intrigued by the way he was gradually drawn out of the world which had previously consumed his life and into the monastery of Gethsemane in Kentucky. When he entered the monastery portico he looked up and engraved in stone were the words, "God alone". To enter this doorway meant your life now is for God without compromise. It already was an invitation to heaven. When I visited Gethsemane monastery many years later, I took delight in finding those iconic words still engraved in stone. I spent a month in the monastery pondering these two words. They sum up everything that it is important for human beings to know. But sadly many do not hear the message. Johannes Hartl, of the Augsburg House of Prayer, after a pilgrimage to various Eastern rite monasteries, including the famous Mt Athos, was confronted with the gospel call to radical discipleship like never before. He was overwhelmed by the stark beauty of "a lifestyle that only makes sense in the light of eternity". He confessed, "the monasteries awakened a longing for eternity in me, and a longing for a place where eternity takes shape".[11] The monastic life lived well is a dramatic sign of this fundamental calling of every human being. Whatever our context, we all need to discover this truth.

When we enter through the doorway of death, and no one can avoid this, we will find ourselves with God alone. We will not be able to lean on our bank account, or our academic degree, or our successful business, or our multiple achievements in art, science, sport, or even ecclesiastical status. We will be with God alone. He is meant to be our last end; caught up in the wonder and beauty of his glory forever. We are created to finish our short life here by entering into the immensity of the ocean of God's love, caught up in the awesome light and splendour of God forever.

The temptation for every one of us is to seek to build our life here as if it will never end. Our time here is passing quickly. We may already enjoy the presence of God now, but this must come to fulfilment. If we become too attached to the things of this world we will lock ourselves into a way of life which enslaves us and makes it impossible for us to attain our eternal destiny. The world offers us possessions, titles, position, status, power and prestige. But all of this will fade in time. The psalmist prays to the Lord, "Make us know the shortness of our life that we may gain wisdom of heart" (Ps 90:12). With admittedly a note of pessimism the psalmist says to the Lord, "You sweep men away like a dream, like grass which springs up in the morning. In the morning it springs up and flowers: by evening it withers and fades" (Ps 90:5-6). A healthy dose of realism is good for the soul. James, when warning the prosperous, who believe they have their life projects planned well ahead cautions the careless, "You never know what will happen tomorrow: you are no more than a mist that is here for a little while and then disappears. The most you can say is: 'If it is the Lord's will, we shall be alive to do this or that'" (James 4:14-15).

We are meant to have Abrahamic faith. Called by the Lord to set out on a journey to a country that the Lord would show him, Abraham obeyed. This land would be his inheritance. But he was given no map. On this pilgrim journey he had to rely on the Lord alone. He had to believe that the promise of the Lord would be fulfilled. On arriving in the land he was not able to possess it, but still had to live in tents waiting for the promise to be fulfilled. It was only fulfilled in the next generation. But as Hebrews comments, "They lived there in tents while he looked forward to a city founded, designed and built by God" (Heb 11:10). And a little later the author adds "in fact they were longing for a better homeland, their heavenly homeland" (Heb 11:16). Faith we are told is "the assurance of things hoped for, and the conviction of things as yet unseen" (Heb 11:1). That is what we need during this short period of time here on earth. While doing all we can to live as true disciples through loving our brothers and sisters in the human race, while giving of ourselves for the sake of others and the betterment of the world, we need to be fully aware that it does not end here. We have to often lift our gaze and listen to the deepest longing of our hearts, and hear the whisper of the Father calling us home to where we most belong.

All of us probably have somewhere which we call our home of origin. We have nostalgic attachment to this place. For some it will be a country town, for others a city suburb, for others maybe another country from which you have come. This is natural and good. Our memories of these places can be mixed, but we know in our heart it is home. Yet, as beautiful as this connection is, we know deep inside that we have been called beyond this place into a greater experience of life. True, some people stay in their original home for their whole life journey. But my point applies to them also. To limit ourselves to our original home can restrict our journey forward. Taking this as an analogy may help to understand my main point when talking about keeping ourselves in the pilgrim state and not settling down. In our spiritual journey we must be always pushing forward, not in our own strength, but as the Lord calls us onwards and upwards. It is a journey of faith, often accompanied by darkness rather than light, but always responding more to the overtures of God pressing in upon us, seeking to persuade and capture us by his love.

Pilgrims have to travel lightly and not settle down anywhere too comfortably. In the gospels we find Jesus constantly disrupting people's lives and calling them to the greater thing. When asked to settle an inheritance battle, he warned, "watch, and be on your guard against avarice of any kind, for a man's life is not made secure by what he owns, even when he has more than he needs". He then told the parable of the man who was doing so well with his crops that he built bigger barns to store the grain (Lk 12:16-21). He said to himself, "My soul, you have plenty of good things laid by for many years to come, take things easy, eat, drink, have a good time". Sounds like a man living out a capitalist dream. But God said to him, "Fool! This very night the demand will be made for your soul; and this hoard of yours, whose will it be then?" Jesus is pointing out the great danger that we can "store up treasure for ourselves rather than make ourselves rich in the sight of God".

There is the rub. We do not know the time or the hour when our earthly pilgrimage will finish. Of course, modern medicine has given us a higher level of predictability, but ultimately it still remains out of our control. With modern technology we are doing all we can to extend the life span, and we can be very grateful for this. Yet the reality of death remains as certain as ever, and its timing still outside our control. There are some people wealthy enough to try and cheat death, by resorting to cryogenics, having their dead bodies frozen in the hope that technology will find a way of resurrection. But it is an expensive form of wishful thinking. The current average life-span for males in Australia is about 80 years and for women a little higher, about 83 years. It is over in a flash, "man who is merely a breath, whose life fades like a passing shadow" (Ps 144:4). We have no abiding city. As another psalm says, "O Lord, you have shown me my end, how short is the length of my days. Now I know how fleeting is my life" (Ps 39:5). We are made for God and our whole existence will come to fruition when our present experience of God comes to full flowering through death; when we encounter the Father, Son and Holy Spirit in eternity.

1
THE MYSTERY OF DEATH

Cultural challenge

Death is the end of our earthly pilgrimage. Its finality is intimidating to most. We spend our lives avoiding its reality. In our Western world, we have fashioned a culture of the comfortable. Our affluence and technology have extended life expectancy, giving us an illusory sense of life forever, or at least for so long in the future that our final exit is not worth contemplating. We find ways to anaesthetise ourselves from death. Funeral parlours, and even Church services can be saccharine affairs, lacking any real perspective of the reality. We talk about people "passing on", a caring euphemism, but often an escape from reality.

For those without the vision of faith, the pursuit of pleasure or endless exciting experiences can dull the awareness of approaching death. Take all the pleasures of the present moment! Fill your life with endless activity! Build your own kingdom! Make yourself rich! Seek fun, fame, fortune! But Jesus warned:

> Do not store up treasure here on earth where moth and woodworm can destroy, and thieves break in and steal; store up treasure in heaven where moth and woodworm cannot destroy and thieves cannot break in and steal. For where your treasure is there will your heart be also (Mt 6:19-21).

For some, the capitalist dream is all consuming. Paul warns us, "The love of money is the source of all evil"! Unfortunately, people fail to realise how temporary this earthly pilgrimage really is. Even good and faithful church-going people live in a haze, seemingly oblivious to the pressing reality of their destiny. An ageing couple I knew who had received a significant pay-out with early retirement from the public service, moved to the coast and spent a couple of years building their dream home, complete with picturesque gardens and fountains. They had just finished the project when she contracted terminal cancer. I visited her in hospital. She took hold of my hand and squeezed tightly. Looking me in the eye with much love she said, "O Ken, we spend so much time in life on things that don't really matter. But there is only one that really does!" I thanked God she had come to that deeper revelation. She had always been a woman of faith, but now as her earthly pilgrimage was winding up she came to a much deeper illumination that ultimately what matters is how we have loved – loved the Lord and loved others.

Atheists or agnostics hope that, even though death will annihilate them, they will live on through their children and the contributions they have made to humanity. With this motivation some can lead very altruistic and unselfish lives. One can imagine God's mercy upon them, but where is the guarantee? Others simply find it hard to face death; there seems to be no redeeming quality. It is not very promising to think of your identity extinguished and your body rotting away in a burial ground. Others unfortunately bring about their own death through despair of life leading to suicide. In this case death is a way out of desperation and unbearable anguish. No one could judge this harshly, but we would surely weep with anguish for such a useless finish to a life with infinite value in the eyes of God. Others in the modern era opt for assisted suicide to escape from what they experience as a hopeless existence of endless suffering. This again is a tragedy, since our human life is given us by God, and we do not have the right to end it by our own hand. The sadness is that many do not realise the depth of human dignity that can be expressed through suffering itself. We live in a society dedicated to the elimination of pain at all costs, but there is another way by which you can become truly human; through surrendering to the Lord in suffering and discovering the deeper mystery of his love as we hang on the cross with him.

Christian death

We know from Genesis that death came into the world as a result of Adam's sin. But we also know from the New Testament that Jesus came to redeem us from sin through his immense love for each of us expressed by his crucifixion. Through his death on the cross he redeemed death. It is no longer a sentence to the darkness of "Sheol" or "Gehenna" as was believed in the Old Testament. When God the Father raised Jesus from the dead not only was sin overcome, but so was the power of death. As Paul cries out triumphantly, "Death! Where is your victory?" (1Cor 15:55)

True Christian death is modelled on that of Jesus. We draw from the grace of his dying on the Cross. We are called to die in Christ. The secret of Jesus' whole life and death was his utter trust in and obedience to the Father. Jesus lived in total solidarity with us, taking our place, and giving us a way back to the Father. When

Jesus cried out on the Cross, "My God, my God, why have you abandoned me" (Mt 27:46) he was articulating the desperate cry of abandonment of the whole of humanity burdened by sin and death. Until this moment, death had been a bottomless cavern of darkness and despair; a terrifying experience of emptiness and annihilation. But with the obedience of Jesus everything was made new. He died with the words, "Father, into your hands I commend my spirit" (Lk 23:46). In solidarity with us, taking our place, he offered the act of obedience on our behalf. This was our redemption! The Father responded by raising him from the dead! Victory over sin and death forever!

The redemption of Jesus has meant a Christian will have three moments of birth! Firstly, being naturally born, crying in the arms of one's mother. The second birthday is baptism, which is a rebirth in the Spirit, by which the child becomes a new creation. We share in the victory of Jesus over sin and death, with the sure promise of resurrection. The third birthday is physical death, which releases God's children from the limitations of this earthly sojourn, allowing the person to go to God into eternal life. Death has its own "birth pangs" but we need not fear them. Our baptism has immersed us into the victory of the death and resurrection of Christ, and if we have lived this dying and rising faithfully, our death, while having the outward features of bodily disintegration, will in fact be a moment of great triumph as we enter into full encounter with God. When we die, we are as helpless and naked as new-born children. But just as a new born child is wrapped in love, so the one who dies in the Lord is enfolded in Love eternal. This is why the days we commemorate the saints is usually not on their initial birthdays, but on the day they died, the time of their entry into glory. It is also why we Christians celebrate in faith the day our loved ones entered into eternal life with God forever.

Victory over death

Returning to the way we are invited to die in Christ, it is good to reflect on his kenosis or self-emptying on the Cross. Jesus did not suffer as a helpless victim who was passively put to death. His life was not taken from him, but he freely gave himself in obedience and love into the Father's hands. This was a free act of self-giving love for all. Jesus, throughout his earthly ministry, entered deeply into the heart of the lostness of humanity. This song of love came to a crescendo on the Cross: "My God, my God, why have you abandoned me?" (Ps 22:1) On the Cross Jesus died in total interior darkness. He experienced unredeemed death that he may redeem it. When Scriptures say he "descended into hell" it means he went into the depth of our sin-spawned humanity, becoming one with the most lost, the poorest of the poor, the loneliest of all human beings. We are told he went to Hades to preach to the "spirits in prison" (1 Pet 3:19), and that God was "freeing him from the pangs of Hades" (Acts 2:24). These biblical images help us to get in touch with the reality that on the Cross Jesus suffered a hell-like agony, but not passively, and without despair. Psalm 22, quoted above, finishes with a song of great hope. He was carving out our way to freedom, so we would not die in despair, but with living hope, no matter how great the darkness.

What Jesus endured on the Cross was unique and unrepeatable. He shouted at the end "It is finished!" (Jn 19:30) The redemption was accomplished. But how can we get in touch with what he experienced on the Cross? I suggest we can understand his suffering not so much by making comparisons about the physical, bodily agony he endured under Roman crucifixion. This was horrendous indeed. But the suffering of his human soul was infinitely more intense. The whole spiritual and moral disfigurement of humankind was laid upon him. As Isaiah said, "He was pierced through for our faults, crushed for our sins. On him lies a punishment that sets us free. By his wounds we are healed" (Is 53:5). Maybe the closest we can come to appreciating this agony is through what John of the Cross calls the "dark night of the spirit", when all intellectual, emotional, and even spiritual supports seem to have evaporated, and the soul is left in a bewildering darkness, feeling itself beyond salvation, but still moving in a persevering faith, regardless of the abandonment. Jesus entered into solidarity with our sinful condition, bearing the agony of death, which is the result of sin. As the Catechism says, "The obedience of Jesus has transformed the curse of death into a blessing".[12]

Our redemption has been accomplished. Death has been overcome. Through our baptism into Christ's death and resurrection we now experience something of the immortality, incorruptibility, and unchangeability of God's love for us. Already we share in the resurrection of Jesus Christ.

> When this perishable nature has put on imperishability, and when this mortal nature has put on immortality, then the words of scripture will come true: Death is swallowed up in victory. Death where is your victory?

Death where is your sting? Now the sting of death is sin, and sin gets its power from the Law. So let us thank God for giving us the victory through our Lord Jesus Christ (1 Cor 15:54-58).

The Holy Spirit within us gives the assurance of the power we need to overcome sin and the fear of death: "And if the Spirit of him who raised Jesus from the dead is living in you, then he who raised Jesus from the dead will give life to your own mortal bodies through the Spirit living in you" (Rom 8:11).

The opinions and fancies of worldly-minded people cannot phase us anymore. All has been accomplished by Jesus. Consequently, Christian funerals are suffused with hope and joy. As the first preface in the funeral liturgy says, "Indeed for your faithful, Lord, life is changed, not ended, and, when this earthly dwelling turns to dust, an eternal dwelling is made ready for them in heaven". We remember how Edith Stein, as a sophisticated Jewish atheist, encountered a widow mourning her husband's untimely death, but with a noticeable difference. This Christian woman had a sure hope and quiet acquiescent peacefulness as she grieved. The joy of the Risen Christ, forever attractive, present in the heart of this widow, intrigued and troubled Edith. Maybe this was real? Edith's heart began to open, and now we celebrate her as St Teresa Benedicta of the Cross, a martyr of Auschwitz. St Paul put it succinctly for those who know the meaning of their rebirth in baptism:

> We believe that having died with Christ we shall return to life with him: Christ, as we know, having been raised from the dead will never die again. Death has no power over

him anymore. When he died, he died, once for all, to sin, so his life now is life with God; and in that way you too must consider yourselves to be dead to sin but alive for God in Christ Jesus (Rom 6:8-11).

Dying in Christ

To be able to enter freely and peacefully into the doorway of death, and to endure whatever suffering it entails, we need to know the good news, which was applied to our lives in baptism. We have this reinforced in our consciousness every time we celebrate Eucharist.

> For anyone who is in Christ, there is a new creation; the old creation has gone, and now the new is here. It is all God's work. It was God who reconciled us to himself through Christ and gave us this work of handing on this reconciliation....and he has entrusted us this news that we are reconciled" (2 Cor 5:17-20).

Pope Francis reflecting on the hour of death sees it as a moment of truth.

> Death lays our life bare. It makes us discover that our acts of pride, of anger and of hate have been in vain: totally in vain. We realize with regret that we have not loved enough and have not sought what was essential. And, on the other hand, we see what we have sown that was truly good: the loved ones for whom we sacrificed ourselves and who now take us by the hand.[13]

I remember a good friend of mine who was dying of cancer and during his life he had fractured relationships with a number of people, and had become alienated from them. He had felt betrayed by others. Just before he died he confided with me that many of these people had come to visit him in his hospital bed. He said, "You know, Fr Ken, as each one entered my room I could see the precious gold in that person." The grace of the eternal perspective! Knowing he was going to God he was able to be reconciled to each person and rejoice in them as a gift from God. Listening to his testimony touched me deeply. I prayed, "Lord, please give me the grace to see the precious gold in each person now! Don't let me wait until the moment of extremity! Help me to live with the eternal perspective now!"

We are to live our lives as servants of the Lord who never go to sleep until the master returns. The world needs our responsibility. Out life is meant to be a labour of love, never lowering our guard, welcoming each new day with wonder, as if it is our last. Every dawn the mercies of the Lord are renewed. We have each day an opportunity to sow seeds for eternity. Pope Francis reminds us:

> Nothing is more important than this appointment with the Lord when he shall come to take us to himself. When that day arrives, we need to be like good servants who spent the night with their loins girt and their lamps burning: we must be ready for the encounter: have you thought of what that encounter with Jesus will be like, when he comes? I trust it will be an embrace, an enormous joy, a great joy! We must live in anticipation of this encounter!"[14]

Trust in God's mercy

When we reflect on our poor lives we can feel we come up short in the light of God's judgement, and wonder whether we will make "it" through the "narrow door" (Lk 13:24). The secret is to put all your trust in God's infinite mercy. Pope Francis urges, "Each time a person, performing the last examination of conscience of his life, discovers that his shortcomings far exceed his good deeds, he must not feel discouraged, but must entrust himself to God's mercy. And this gives us hope; it opens the heart![15] At the hour of death we ought to repeat the word of the repentant criminal who turned to Jesus who was hanging on the Cross next to him, "Jesus, remember me". With these words we can gain the assurance given to the criminal, "This day you will be with me in paradise" (Lk 23:43).

This encounter of mercy on Calvary, when Jesus promises eternity in heaven to the repentant criminal is the only time that the word "paradise" is used in the gospels. It was reserved for a major sinner at the hour of death. Our true condition before God is like this man, utterly in need of God's mercy. He is always won by our heartfelt plea for mercy, just like in the parable of the tax-collector at the back of the Temple. This is the message of God given through St Faustina, "Let the greatest sinners place their trust in my mercy. They have the right before others to trust in the abyss of my mercy … I cannot punish even the greatest sinner if he makes an appeal to my compassion; on the contrary, I justify him in my unfathomable and inscrutable mercy."[16]

Pope Francis assures us, "Paradise is not a fairytale place, much less an enchanted garden. Paradise is the embrace of God, infinite love, and we enter there thanks to Jesus, who died on the cross for us."[17] At the hour of our death, no matter what the circumstances, whether we are surrounded by loved ones, or abandoned and bereft of human contact, Jesus will be there beside us. He will come to take us to the most beautiful place of all. Like Simeon, who had spent a life-time in obedience to God, we will be able to say, "Lord, now let your servant depart in peace, according to your word; for my eyes have seen your salvation" (Lk 2:29-30). At that moment, all confusion will vanish. All earthly realities will be passing away - our achievements, insights, relationships, even spiritual gifts will fade. But we will not weep, since we are entering into an encounter with Christ that will last forever. Love will endure, since "love never ends" (1 Cor 13:8).

Surrender to the Father

The secret to a 'happy death' is to live every moment of one's life for God. The more we fall in love with him, overwhelmed by his intensely personal love for us, the more we be able to love others in a real and practical way. The more his love infuses our soul, the more we will walk securely through any dark moment of life, and ultimately the dark passageway of death. Just as Jesus surrendered to the Father on our behalf effecting our redemption as he died on the cross, we seek to die in union with him. Whenever the hour of death comes, we will be called to give our lives over into the Father's hands and trust in his infinite love.

Thérèse of Lisieux is a beautiful example for us. When the time had come at the age of 25 years to return to God, she was ready. In fact, she was eager for the consummation of her life. Earlier as a novice she had written, "We must see life in its true light, it is an instant between two eternities."[18] She pondered deeply on life and its meaning. Having surprising insight for someone so young, she wrote:

> Yes life is a treasure – each instant is an eternity, an eternity of joy for heaven, and eternity...to see God face to face, to be simply one with him! Only Jesus is, everything else is not … life will be short, eternity has no end. Let every instant of our life be for Him alone. Let creatures touch us only in passing. There is but one thing to do during the night of this life, that single night which will come but once, and that is to love, to love Jesus with all the strength of our heart, and to save souls for Him that he might be loved.[19]

Then three months before her death, suffering from acute tuberculosis, Thérèse speaks of her readiness for death:

> What attracts me to the Homeland of Heaven is … the hope that I may at last love Him as I have so longed to love Him and the thought that I shall bring a multitude of souls to love Him, who will bless Him for all eternity.[20]

Thérèse had a deep desire to die for love. She originally thought that this would mean being consumed by such a fire that she would have "sublime impulses and delightful encounters of love". But as things turned out she was destined to have excruciatingly painful sickness over many months. She realised that "to die with love" was a higher sacrifice when there was no sweetness, but simply the total gift of herself in self-emptying love. She was drawn ever more deeply into the experience of the crucified one. She could see that to die in love, which was her aim, was not to experience mystical transports, but to share in the darkness of his agony. The death of love that she desired was really that of Jesus on the Cross. She wanted to truly appear before God "with empty hands".[21]

Early Christian martyrs

The early Christian martyrs witness to the victory of Christ most powerfully. In the ancient world death was a terrifying prospect and the after-life full of shrouded mystery. In the Roman Empire people worshipped pagan gods, including Hades who they believed ruled the Underworld. On the edge of the Underworld the dead spirits were met by a ferryman who moved them across the river Styx from the land of the living to the land of the dead. There they faced judgement. The good went to Elysium and the bad were thrown to the pit of Tartarus, and the mediocre (the majority) drifted aimlessly around the City of Pluto. This offered maybe some degree of comfort for the dying, but most lived in terror of the dark room of death. Elaborate funeral rites with professional mourners were celebrated to induce the gods to ensure a good fate for the dead person. They even placed a coin on or in the dead person's mouth so that the soul could pay Charon, the ferryman, to take them across the River Styx. If for some reason they did not make it across the Styx, they were lost in a shadowy existence forever.

The vast majority of people in these ancient times feared what awaited them. They shrank back from death which had no hope and nothing to desire. Then Jesus came. That changed everything. The Christians did not fear death. St Athanasius declared:

> Everyone is by nature afraid of death and of bodily dissolution. The marvel of marvels, is that the one who is enfolded in the faith of the cross despises this natural fear, and for the sake of the cross is no longer cowardly in the face of it.[22]

Christians lived by their faith in Christ risen from the dead. He had overcome the power of death.

Death was no longer ultimate distress and destruction, but joyful resurrection and joining Christ in eternal life. We think of the famous Ignatius of Antioch (+108AD), chained as he said to "savage leopards"; meaning the ten Roman soldiers, who were taking him to Rome to be fed to the lions. He writes to the Christian community in Rome begging them not to interfere. He had no fear of death, but desired the privilege of martyrdom, to die in ultimate imitation of the death of Jesus, and to win the crown of everlasting glory:

> I must implore you to do me no untimely kindness; pray leave me to be a meal for the beasts, for it is they who can provide my way to God. I am His wheat, ground fine by the lion's teeth to be made purest bread for Christ.[23]

What was happening in this man? Filled with zeal for the kingdom of God he knew that his death would not only be a victory for him personally, but also for the Church under persecution. This witness to the resurrection of Jesus spoke more powerfully than a thousand sermons. He was willing to die to himself so that Christ may be given the glory. "Here and now, as I write in the fullness of life, I am yearning for death with all the passion of a lover. Earthly longings have been crucified; in me here is left no spark of desire for mundane things, but only a murmur of living water that whispers within me, 'Come to the Father'"[24]

St Athanasius marvels at this wonderful resurrection faith in ordinary Christians. He says that before Jesus "the holiest of men were afraid of death, and mourned the dead as those who perish". But he declares:

> Now that the Saviour has raised his body, death is no longer terrible, but all who believe in Christ tread it underfoot as nothing, and prefer to die rather than to deny their faith in Christ, knowing full well that when they die they do not perish, but live indeed and become incorruptible through resurrection.[25]

Add to this the martyrdom of thousands of men, women and children in those early years of witness to the resurrection of Jesus. Another example would be Saints Felicity and Perpetua who were put to death in Carthage in AD203. Felicity was pregnant when arrested and Perpetua was nursing her infant son. Felicity would have been spared martyrdom if she was still pregnant. But she prayed to be able to deliver the child early so she could have the crown of martyrdom. Her prayers were answered and both children were given into care of the Christian community. The two valiant women entered the arena joyfully and with shining faces. Perpetua sang psalms, and when the crowd demanded they be scourged first, the women thanked God to be able to share more closely in the passion of the Master. They were finished off by swords. Perpetua showed her courage when she guided the novice swordsman to set the blade upon her neck.[26]

Another example I can't restrain myself from mentioning is Polycarp, bishop of Smyrna. He had been a disciple of John the Apostle before John was exiled to Patmos. No doubt Polycarp often meditated on the words of John written from Patmos to the Church of Smyrna, and recorded in the book of Revelations: "Be faithful unto death and I will give you the crown of life" (Rev 2:10). He was destined to respond to this exhortation in an amazingly courageous way. At the age of 86 years, Polycarp, the revered bishop of Smyrna, was arrested. When the Roman police arrived at his door late at night he was in bed in the attic. They had been tipped off as to his whereabouts by a house-boy who had confessed under torture. They now had their man. As soon as he heard them arrive he went downstairs to greet them graciously and to order them food and drink. He then requested an hour to pray, knowing he was heading towards his execution. They granted this. He stood up, lifted his hands in prayer, and stayed there for two hours. This somewhat unnerved his captors! But they still took him to the station and then to the arena. The Governor in the arena tried to persuade him to recant. "Why not just say, 'Caesar is Lord!' That's not too hard to say! Have respect for your age! Revile your Christ!" Polycarp's reply was, "For eighty-six years I have served him, and he has done me no wrong. How can I blaspheme my King and my Saviour?" The Governor threatened him with fire, rather than the beasts, for which Polycarp had already shown disdain. Polycarp replied, "The fire you threaten me with cannot go on burning for very long; after a while it will go out. But what you are unaware of are the flames of future judgement and everlasting torment which are in store for the ungodly". So, he was burnt alive, but since his body seemed resistant to the flames, they eventually stabbed him to death. Eye-witnesses say there was a sweet smell of incense emanating from his charred body. How these early martyrs show us the way to die!

But then what of the thousands of martyrs down through the centuries and other holy people who have gone to death with such equanimity because they knew it was a glorious day of being reborn in Christ. We look to the martyrs because they model to us the truth that death is no longer a disaster, no matter what the circumstances, but entry into fullness of life with God forever. Death has been redeemed from fear of dissolution and despair by the victory of Jesus. All who are united with him in faith experience death as a victory in him, leading to a share in his resurrection forever. Maximilian Kolbe comes to mind as a quintessential example of this. In Auschwitz concentration camp a prisoner had escaped. The other prisoners from his cell block were punished by being forced to stand in the boiling sun all day long.

Then at sunset the Nazis began arbitrarily selecting 10 men for the starvation bunker.[27] One of them burst into tears, "How I pity my wife and children whom I'm leaving as orphans". All were frozen with fear. Except one. Maximilian broke ranks and came before the commander. "What does this Polish swine want?" Fritsch demanded. Kolbe answered, "I want to die in place of this one condemned". Fritsch asked, "Who are you?". He answered, "I am a Catholic priest". That was enough for Fritsch. As far as he was concerned, priests were the scum of the earth. The ten men, condemned to death, were marched toward their death cell. But as time went on this bunker was different from all previously. Under Kolbe's calm guidance and loving words they learnt to pray and to sing songs to the Lord and to the Blessed Virgin Mary. He taught them how to die without fear. Finally, after three weeks, he was the last to die, having been ministered an injection of carbolic acid. One of the guards testified after the war that when he was sent to carry out Maximilian's body he found him sitting on the floor leaning against the wall with his eyes wide open. His body was clean and radiant. His face was bright and serene.[28]

Maximilian Kolbe's death is a beautiful imitation of the death of Jesus, "No greater love has any man than to lay down his life for his friends" (Jn 15:13). He deliberately modelled his death on that of Jesus and drew all his strength from his Master. His death speaks the truth that ultimately it is love that matters, and every death in Christ is a victory for love.

2
JUDGEMENT

Pope John Paul II taught that mercy is the most stupendous attribute of God.[29] Similarly, St Faustina Kowalska declared that mercy is the "highest quality in the heart of God".[30] This is the God we preach. We know that he will never give up on us, no matter how far we go from him. We know he is the Good Shepherd who has the strange economy of leaving the ninety-nine to go seeking the lost one. He is the loving Father who waits patiently for the return of his wayward son, and runs to him and throws his arms around him and kisses him tenderly (Lk 15:11-24). He is the "hound of heaven". No matter where we go, he will be there to call us to himself. Even when we run away in the opposite direction, like Jonah, he pursues us, and providentially makes it possible for us to do what otherwise we would not have done (Jonah 3:1-3). He sent his only Son to become one of us and to die in atonement for our sins on calvary, and then marvellously raised him from the dead. His saving love and mercy is all abounding. But now we must talk about his judgement!

The Church teaches that, after we die, we will be brought before Christ as judge of our lives. Consequently, our souls will either go to heaven immediately (possibly after a time of purification in purgatory), or they will go to hell. This encounter with Christ immediately after dying is called the "particular judgement" to distinguish it from the "final judgement" which will occur when the Lord comes again on the last day. While on the last day the Lord will come in sovereignty, our eternal destiny is determined immediately upon death. Then when the Lord returns on the last day, he will bring about the general resurrection. All those still on earth will be transformed body and soul by resurrection power, and all souls in heaven and hell will be reunited with their bodies. That is when all will stand before the judgement seat of God and the life of everyone will be made manifest.

In recent years many theologians have questioned the separation of the soul from the body in the period between death and the final resurrection of the body. They suggest this teaching was formulated from the false Greek notion of a dualism of body and soul. They argue that it makes no sense for the body to be without the soul, nor for the soul to be wandering unattached from the body. The official Church has sought to clarify this confusion. The problem is that some thinkers tend to equate what the Church calls "the soul" to inadequate concepts from ancient Greek philosophy. The Church means by the soul "the person with consciousness and will", in other words the "human self". So, the Church teaches that "the soul" which leaves the body at death is definitely the personal self, not something less than the person. However, only at the time of the general resurrection from the dead will the soul and body be reunited. At that point the *whole* human person will be like the resurrected body of Christ.[31]

The Teaching of Jesus

Most of the judgement texts in the Scriptures refer to the final judgement. But it is clear also that judgement immediately follows death, and there is no possibility of repentance after death. As Hebrews says, "Men only die once and after that comes judgement, so Christ, too, offers himself only once to take the faults of many on himself, and when he appears a second time, it will not be to deal with sin but to reward with salvation those who are waiting for him" (Heb 9:28). So, the judgement made at death holds for eternity. The texts in the gospels on judgement are strong and function as warnings to amend our lives before it is too late. Jesus makes many illusions to this day of reckoning. He urges his listeners, "Try your best to enter by the narrow door. I tell you, many will try to enter and will not succeed" (Lk 13:24). The meaning here is to thrust yourself vigorously through the narrow door. It is a call for decisiveness and determination, a single-minded focus on the kingdom. He continues to warn that many will come from east and west to take their place in the kingdom of God, but "the subjects of the kingdom will be turned out into the dark where there will be weeping and grinding of teeth" (Mt 8:12). He makes it clear that on judgement day those who thought they were virtuous because of their religious practices may not hear favourable words, and those who are despised publicly now may be found worthy. He warns the chief priests and pharisees, "I tell you solemnly, tax collectors and prostitutes are making their way into the kingdom of God before you" (Mt 21:31).

When lamenting the lack of conversion of Chorazin and Bethsaida, Jesus says, "I tell you that it will not go as hard on judgement day with Tyre and Sidon as with you" (Mt 11:22-23). Again, speaking harshly to a culture which has rejected him he warns, "On judgement day the men of Nineveh will stand up with this generation and condemn it, because when Jonah preached they repented, and there is something greater than Jonah here" (Mt 12:41). These are only a couple of many texts on judgement that appear throughout the gospels. All the passages warning about judgement are intended to shake us out of our torpor, to call us to repent, seeking genuine conversion of heart before it is too late. They aim to call people to a decision. They are signposts, alerting us to danger, challenging us to change our hearts before time runs out. They do not convey a message to be feared, but function as a sign of hope. These texts encourage us to trust in God's mercy. They put hell before our eyes as a real danger; they intend to affirm beyond doubt that it really is possible to miss the whole point of human existence. We could wilfully ignore God's call to salvation. Through our own foolishness we could damn ourselves to lose God forever. The strong sayings of Jesus encourage us to wake up from our sloth and set our hearts on the kingdom of God and his righteousness before it is too late.

Pope Francis encourages us "not to grow weary of keeping watch over our thoughts and our attitudes, in order that we may be given even now a foretaste of the warmth and splendour of God's Face – and this will be beautiful – which in eternal life we shall contemplate in all its fullness."[32] He encourages us to walk without fear by submitting ourselves regularly to self-examination and turning to the Lord for forgiveness of our sins. If we live this way we will surely be brought to the glory of heaven.

The clearest and most dramatic example of these warning texts is when, referring to the last day, Jesus declares, "When the Son of Man comes in glory, escorted by all the angels, then he will take his seat on his throne of glory … he will separate people one from another as a shepherd separates sheep from goats." The king will say to the "sheep" on his right "Come you whom my Father has blessed, take your heritage the kingdom prepared for you since the foundation of the world. For I was hungry, and you gave me food; I was thirsty and you gave me to drink; I was a stranger and you welcomed me; naked and you clothed me; sick and you visited me; in prison and you came to see me". And "the virtuous" will ask when they did all this. He will answer, "In so far as you did it to the least of my brethren you did it to me". On the other hand, those who neglected to do these acts of mercy are told, "Go away from me, with your curse upon you, to eternal fire prepared for the devil and his angels" (Mt 25:11-44).

Reflecting on this text, Pope Francis reminds us "At the end of our life we will be judged on love, that is, on our concrete commitment to love and serve Jesus in our littlest and neediest brothers and sisters. That mendicant, that needy person who reaches out his hand is Jesus; that sick person whom I must visit is Jesus; that inmate is Jesus, that hungry person is Jesus."[33] Now is the time for a change of heart and opening our lives in practical love for others.

Facing the reality and trusting in God's mercy

In the modern era we are shy about judgement. We rather turn to more comforting texts that clearly indicate it is God's will to save everyone. Paul says, "God our saviour wants everyone to be saved and reach full knowledge of the truth" (1Tim 2:4). Jesus said, "I have come not to condemn the world, but to save the world" (Jn 12:47). And Jesus promised, "When I am lifted up from the earth, I will draw all to myself" (Jn 12:32). Paul expressed this in a hymn exalting Jesus: "every knee shall bow, in heaven and earth and the underworld, and every tongue confess that Jesus Christ is Lord to the glory of God the Father" (Phil 2:10-11). Paul also spoke of the whole of history in some way culminating in Christ; "he would bring everything together under Christ as head, everything in the heavens and everything on earth" (Eph 1:10).

These all-inclusive texts are important and must be held before our eyes always. But we would be foolish to dismiss the texts on judgment. It would be presumptuous and hence sinful against genuine hope if we took the attitude that I don't need to change. We are tempted to say to ourselves, "somehow everything will turn out all right". In this context I have heard the well-known saying of Julian of Norwich, "All will be well" blithely misquoted. From the scriptural evidence and the teaching of the Church such banal optimism would seem foolhardy and not helpful in sharing the true gospel message. On the other hand, there are some Catholics, maybe a dwindling number, who are still holding firmly to a rendition of the gospel message which maximises fear of judgement and the punishment of hell-fire. It's important to find a way through this polarisation between naïve optimism and sheer pessimism. I want to make just a few observations that hopefully will help.

There is absolutely no question that God is love, and his will is that all men and women be saved through his mercy. Most importantly, the judge of our lives is Jesus, our Saviour and Lord. We have known his mercy again and again. We can be absolutely sure that he is a *merciful* judge. This makes all the difference. While we must not be presumptuous, we know that in the heart of Jesus his mercy has primacy over his justice. We can gain hope from a beautiful text in Hosea. The Lord is bemoaning the unfaithfulness of his people, falling back into idolatry again and again: "My people are diseased through their disloyalty; they call on Baal, but he does not cure them". The Lord is, as it were, tempted to smite them. But he relents, "Ephraim, how could I part with you? Israel, how could I give you up?" He wonders whether he could treat them with vengeance, but says, "My heart recoils from it, my whole being trembles at the thought. I will not give rein to my fierce anger. I will not destroy Ephraim again: I am the Holy One in your midst and I have no wish to destroy you" (Hos 11:7-9). This text depicts, in a dramatic way, the struggle in the heart of God between his mercy and his justice; in the end his mercy trumps his justice.

Another helpful text is found in James: "there will be judgement without mercy for those who have not been merciful themselves, but the merciful need have no fear of judgement" (James 2:13). This underlines that God is mercy. What matters is that we have a merciful heart towards others and act with mercy. It fits with the text from Matthew mentioned earlier where Jesus says, "As often as you did it to the least of my brethren you did it to me".

The gift of free will

As an expression of his love and mercy God has given us freedom. "He does not want to ambush us mortals or bypass our freedom.

Our eternal destiny depends on our decision and our response to God's love".[34] While the Lord will pursue us and give us a thousand second chances, he will never force our response. It is possible for people to ignore or reject his approach. To definitively reject God's love is by definition the loss of eternal beatitude. We call that awful reality hell. God who created us without our cooperation, does not intend to save us without our cooperation. While he definitely wills our salvation he does not will it without our personal involvement. It is a decision for life or for death. It is sobering to recall that there is no repentance after death. At that point, the die has been cast.

The text where Jesus speaks of the two paths is critical for us to ponder. "Enter by the narrow gate, since the road to perdition is wide and spacious, and many take it; but it is a narrow gate and a hard road that leads to life, and only a few take it" (Mt 7:13-14). This text is not meant to give us ammunition to declare most people will take the 'wide and spacious' path to hell. It is not for us to make that calculation. Judging is God's business. The text is rather a call to decision. We need to cut out all those worldly things which set our path towards perdition. We must embrace the cross of Jesus and die to ourselves in following him with perseverance. Another text which supports this decisiveness in discipleship is from Deuteronomy, "See today I set before you life or death, blessing or curse. Choose life, then, so that you and your descendants may live in the love of the Lord your God, obeying his voice, clinging to him, for in this your life consists, and on this depends your long stay in the land" (Deut 30: 19-20).

Do not be afraid

There is no need for us to be afraid of death and judgement. Hold to the Lord in your life and he will hold you at the moment of your extremity. I remember an elderly woman who was on the point of death. Visiting her for the last time I brought her as usual Holy Communion, so she could receive, Jesus, the Bread of life. Even though she was dozing in a semi-conscious state, as soon as she saw the pyx in which I was carrying the host she sat up in the bed with her hands stretched out to welcome her Lord. With a radiant face she kept repeating, "Jesus, thank you!" Already she was preparing for the ultimate encounter with her Saviour and Lord. When our lives are in union with the Lord, the end may be physically painful, as it was for this lady; the body may be breaking down, but the spirit is awake, ready for the ultimate moment of one's journey, the moment of truth, when we hear the whisper, "The Master is here!" (Jn 11:28)

Priests have the privilege of attending many people who are in their dying days. We are more than often inspired by their faith, resignation, and peacefulness of heart. Recently I was at the bedside of a faithful woman dying after a long battle with multiple sclerosis. I knew her journey well. She had lived for the Lord and was deeply surrendered to his will. Now she was in her final hours. I was able to anoint her and minister Viaticum, which is Holy Communion given to assist the dying to journey through the door of death with confidence and courage. After receiving Communion, seemingly from nowhere she found the words to utter quite vigorously, "I am so privileged to have Jesus come to me to take me home". Such a beautiful and inspiring response!

She knew she was going home to the Father's house, that a place had been prepared for her by Jesus, and he was coming to take her home.

I was reading recently of a young monk named Vincent who had joined the Canons Regular at the Lagrasse Abbey in France in 2007.[35] He already had early signs of sclerosis, but was still accepted into the monastery. After a few years his condition worsened. He was hospitalised for a while in a health centre specialising in multiple sclerosis. Typically, in his youthful enthusiasm, he did all he could to convert the medical team. But there was nothing much the team could do with his physical state. He returned home to the monastery and the monks decided they would keep him there and accompany him until his death. But they could do very little for him, except help him deal practically with his physical disability as the disease increasingly took control of his body.

At the appropriate moment, he was allowed to profess his final vows. Even at that point there was already a grave dug at the back of the monastery ready to receive him. Monks tend to be very practical about life and death. Vincent rejoiced in being able to spend time with nature, but after a while this was less possible as his body was deteriorating more. But nothing was going to kill his spirit. One day Vincent let one of his confidantes know, "I have just asked God to be able to go quickly to heaven. But I told him to do as he pleased". A beautiful prayer of surrender! His one fear was that he would die during a choking fit. What could be worse than dying of suffocation? Vincent often said to his brothers who loved him greatly, "I gave everything to Jesus. He has taken everything. I thank him".

At his death Father Emmanuel-Marie, the superior, asked Vincent's mother to take his right hand and his sister his left. Father Emmanuel related, "The little brother seemed more at rest, carried away on a journey that transcended him. We were certain he was going to leave us. He had become transparent. The times of crises, the times of suffocations went away. He was no longer swimming in that ocean of suffering which was his prison. Brother Vincent had no fear. His departure was sweet. The day before, spasms had distorted his face. At the hour of death, he was radiant".

The brothers all gathered around him. The last breath, the last look, the last beating of his heart had an air of victory. The brothers were crying and praying at the same time.

My dear friends, this humble death in an obscure monastery went unnoticed by the world, but it spoke of truth, that our time here on earth is short and has one ultimate purpose, to give glory to God, and on this we will be judged. May you, like Vincent, have no fear of judgement.

3
THE COMMUNION OF SAINTS

God has created us in relationship with one another. No one is meant to live in isolation, disconnected from others. The Covid restrictions have made us more aware than ever of our need to be connected for the sake of our humanity. In the beginning, when humanity fell, as related in Genesis, the rebellion against God led to dislocation in relationships. Jealousy, bitterness, hatred and revenge splintered the original unity. The story of the Tower of Babel depicts the pride and hubris of humanity towards God, leading to a split into alien groupings seemingly unable to communicate and move together. The original communion was lost. So, when God began to move in human history to bring about our salvation he began to communicate himself to a people, not just to particular individuals. He chose the people of Israel, called them, consecrated them to him, and forged a covenant with them. No one would be saved alone. God's saving action with the human race happens through forming a people. He intends that ultimately all men and women will be brought together in relationship with him and hence in communion with one another.

The Church: sign and means of unity

When God became a man in Jesus Christ, born of Mary in a stable in Bethlehem, he was committing himself to humanity in an extraordinary way. By becoming one of us he was making it possible for all of humanity to be reconciled with God and with one another again. This gift of reconciliation was attained definitively when Jesus gave of himself for us on the cross. In solidarity with the whole of humanity he bore our sin and broke its power, restoring again the possibility of communion with one another. He founded his Church as the sign and instrument of this new communion of all human beings. The Church would be the ordinary means by which salvation will come to the whole world. All men and women are meant to encounter Christ as their Saviour and Lord through the Church's preaching and being incorporated into the Church's life. It certainly shows the fragility of God's plan for the salvation of humanity when we consider it is in the hands of his Church. We have to put our faith in God that he knows what he is doing, and that despite all our sinfulness and failures, his power will work through our weakness. "We are only the earthenware jars that hold this treasure, to make it clear that such an overwhelming power comes from God and not from us" (2 Cor 4:7).

God's work of salvation through Jesus Christ is intended to be spearheaded by his Church. The community of the Church is meant to be a sign and means for people to find their way to heaven. But before talking about heaven, let's first consider the broad teaching on the communion of saints. For many Catholics the term, communion of saints, refers exclusively to the saints in heaven. We are used to talking about "saints" as canonised men and women who have lived amazingly heroic lives for God. But when we confess in the Creed our belief in the communion of saints, we actually mean the communion of all those in Christ here on earth, those in purgatory, and also those in heaven. Pope Paul VI's *Credo of the People of God* states:

> I believe in the communion of all the faithful of Christ, those who are pilgrims on earth, the dead who are being purified, and the blessed in heaven, all together forming one Church; and we believe that in this communion, the merciful love of God and of his saints is always attentive to our prayers.[36]

The Body of Christ

We are one body, the Body of Christ. This teaching has its origin in the experience of St Paul on the road to Damascus (Acts 9:1-19). Paul (who was then still going by the name of Saul) was making his way to Damascus to arrest the followers of 'The Way' i.e., Christians. Suddenly he encountered the glory of the risen Christ and was thrown to the ground by the extraordinary impact of the vision. He heard the words, "Saul, Saul, why are you persecuting me?" Saul asked, "Who are you Lord?" The voice answered, "I am Jesus, and you are persecuting me". Saul could well have replied, "I am not persecuting you, but your followers". But, as he pondered these words through three days of darkness before his baptism by Ananias, their significance must have struck him deeply. To touch the followers of Christ was to touch the risen Christ in whom they found their identity. From this experience Paul developed his teaching that followers of Jesus are baptised into Christ, that is they become members of Christ's Body. Later he used the analogy of the human body to explain this communion with Christ, which makes us the Church. He wrote to the Romans, "Just as each of our bodies has several parts and each part has a separate function, so all of us, in union with Christ, form one body, and as parts we belong to each other" (Rom 12: 4-5).

Paul's teaching gave Christians their identity. "In the one Spirit we were all baptised, Jews as well as Greeks, slaves as well as citizens, and one Spirit was given to all to drink" (1 Cor 12:13). To be baptised is to be grafted onto the Body of Christ; our new personal identity as a Christian comes from belonging to his Body. He insisted that, just as in the human body, no part of the Body of Christ can claim to be self-sufficient. All the parts of the body serve the good of the whole, and each part has different gifts for the sake of the whole. This way of thinking is very different from the individualistic way of thinking today. The contemporary concept of "Jesus and me", a unique relationship cut off from the Church, is alien to Paul; a totally unscriptural stance. Paul insists, "Now you together are Christ's body; but each of you is a different part of it" (1 Cor 12:27).

Discovering our place in the Body

We can belong to many groups, societies and organisations in life, but none is so fundamental and unique as finding membership in the Church, the Body of Christ. When Bill Hayden, in 1987 was being sworn into office as Governor General of Australia, he would not put his hand on the bible, since he was a publicly professed atheist. He had renounced his childhood Catholic upbringing during his public life. Yet his Christian formation was still manifest in his heart for the disadvantaged and the needy. During his political career he was an enthusiastic advocate for the poor. He championed the introduction of universal medical coverage for all Australians. Then, after retirement, in 2018, much to the surprise of many, he requested baptism in the Catholic church. Bill attributes his years of atheism to a number of factors. His father was an atheist and violent at home. His mother was a staunch Catholic and he has good memories of her love and care. He attended Catholic primary school, but as he entered his teens he became sceptical. At religion class in high school Bill protested against the veracity of some of the bible stories which seemed unreal. He also reacted against the perceived wealth of the Church. Then later in life a major factor for his refusal to believe in God was the loss of their five-year-old daughter. She had been accidentally knocked down by a car. Bill could not find peace in prayer, even though he was advised to turn to God. He recalls being assisted by a good, young priest who was trying to help him deal with his grief. But he reacted negatively to people who would say "It is all God's will; you just have to accept it". He could not reconcile this loss with the concept of a good God.

During the Parliamentary debate around the Medicare legislation, Bill had been approached by Sister Angela Mary Doyle, the administrator of the Mater Hospital. She joined him and gave moral support to his cause. It developed into a 40-year friendship. He admired her courage and love for the poor. He recalls "I've always felt embraced and loved by her Christian example".[37] Then when he visited her in hospital after she had suffered a heart-attack he came away deeply moved. He shared with his wife he knew he had undoubtedly been with "a holy person". While reading a book on Islam, he decided that Islam was a religion of rules, but the heart of Christianity was about love. Writing to his friends after his baptism Bill revealed he could not stand the emptiness any longer, "There's been a gnawing pain in my heart and soul about what is the meaning of life. What's my role in it?" To one of his closest friends he disclosed, "I couldn't bear the emptiness without belief. I can no longer accept that human existence is self-sufficient and isolated".

Bill rejoiced in being welcomed into the Church community. Drawn by love, stirred by questions of meaning, seeking to fill a gnawing emptiness, he allowed himself to be embraced by the communion of God's people. Asked by reporters why he would do this in the midst of the clerical abuse crisis, Bill replied people need to look at their faith in Christ, which is found in the Church, not at "agents" of the Church who are often blatantly sinful. Now in his eighties Bill is aware that the end of his earthly journey is close. Reconciled to God, he has a new peace and serenity of heart and is ready to meet the Lord whenever he comes.

A communion of relationships

As we saw earlier the Catechism teaches that the communion of saints is comprised of all the members of Christ's Body; those on the pilgrim journey here on earth, those being purified in purgatory, and those glorified in heaven. There is a communion of love and holiness, albeit very imperfect, shared by all in the pilgrim Church on earth. This continues after death. From very early in the Church there was a solid belief that the saints, apostles, martyrs and confessors were not separated from the pilgrim church through death. Rather, they believed firmly that all members of the Body of Christ, whether on earth or in life after death, remain joined to those still on their earthly pilgrimage. They were not only joined to Christ as Head, but also to all members of his Body in the church on earth. Those who have gone before, especially those recognised officially as having attained eternal glory, were called upon to help those still needing healing and growth in holiness here on earth.

Those who are still in the state of purification in purgatory experience this ecclesial solidarity when we pray for them in our liturgies, or in private prayer, when we remember them and offer up sacrifices for them. Pope John Paul II sought to clarify the status of those in purgatory:

> They are not separated from God but immersed in the love of Christ. They are neither separated from the saints in heaven, who are already enjoying fullness of eternal life; nor are they separated from us on earth – who continue on our pilgrim journey to the Father's house. We all remain united in the Mystical Body of Christ, and we can therefore offer up prayers and good works on behalf of our brothers and sisters in purgatory.[38]

The pilgrim Church on earth has always looked to the inspiring example of the blessed, especially the formally recognised saints and martyrs, and the Blessed Virgin Mary. Through their example we are inspired to keep our focus on our heavenly homeland, and imitate the way they walked in holiness, showing the way for us to follow Jesus. With such a great "cloud of witnesses" (Heb 12:1) we are less likely to lose our way. We cherish the memory of the saints who have gone before us due to their amazing example of how to live the gospel.

We also turn to the saints in heaven for help. We gain the assistance we need to set our hearts on the kingdom of God with unswerving fervour. We rely upon their prayers. John Paul II explains:

> Being more closely united to Christ, those who dwell in heaven consolidate the holiness of the whole church ... Once received into their heavenly home and being present to the Lord (see 2 Cor 5:8), through him and with him and in him they do not cease to intercede with the Father for us, as they proffer the merits which they acquired on earth through the one mediator between God and humanity, Christ Jesus ... So by their familial concern is our weakness greatly helped.[39]

Saints in heaven want to help us

The union with the saints in heaven is through the love that is found in Christ. If we love one another then God's love is perfected in us (1 Jn 4:12). The saints in heaven are constantly entering more deeply into the experience of the infinite love of God. Consequently, they share in his love for all of us pilgrims still struggling on our earthly journey towards heaven. Many of the saints have expressed their wish that in the life to come they would spend themselves helping those left behind on earth. When St Dominic was dying, his brothers were deeply grieved by the prospect of losing him. But he assured them, "Do not weep, for I shall be more useful to you after my death and I shall help you then more effectively than during my life". Through the love of the saints we are strengthened on our journey. Our communion with the saints joins us more deeply in union with Christ, and deepens us in holiness.

St Thérèse of Lisieux, towards the end of her short life, told her sisters, "I want to spend my heaven doing good on earth".[40] She had a spiritual friendship with a young priest, Maurice Bellière, who was struggling to believe in God's love and had sought her intercession to be able to trust in his mercy. They had never met in person, but their conversation by letter witnesses to a genuine love that was to endure beyond the grave. Maurice had received news that Thérèse was close to death due to the onslaught of tuberculosis. In what he thought was his last letter to her Maurice expresses his deep grief in losing her. But he reminds her that she promised to be with him in eternal life, "Your soul will guide mine, speak to it and console it ... little Sister ... Having now become His spouse and reigning with Him, you will win my cause and draw me to Him on the last day."[41]

Thérèse in reply wanted Maurice to know she will be watching over him, and will help him discover more the tender mercy of God. "When I shall come into port I shall teach you, dear little brother of my soul, how you must sail the stormy sea of the world, with the abandon and love of a child who knows that his Father cherishes him, and would never think of leaving him alone in the hour of danger ...".[42] She was keen to assure him that her going to God would not sever the relationship. Rather, entry into heaven would increase her capacity to help him by her prayerful presence to walk in her "little way", knowing the tenderness and mercy of God. "But I am sure that I shall greatly help you to walk more surely by his delightful way once I have been delivered from my mortal envelope; and soon you will say like St Augustine: 'Love is the weight that pulls me forward'."[43]

4
HEAVEN

Ideas about heaven abound, but they inevitably fall far short of the reality. For some it is a perfect day at the golf-course, or uninterrupted physical sensation, or a party with family and friends, or a happy hunting ground. Others may see it as the reign of perfect peace on earth, or the universal experience of social justice. Others may speak of it as simply the ecstasy of my heart when things come together so well.

The new atheists simply eliminate heaven from all rational thinking. Stephen Hawkins, the legendary scientist, who lived for decades with the prospect of death hanging over his head due to his life-long condition, insisted he was not afraid of death, but dismissed heaven as a fairy tale. In an interview with the *Guardian* in 2011 he confidently announced, "I regard the brain as a computer which will stop working when its components fail. There is no heaven or afterlife for broken down computers; that is a fairy story for people who are afraid of the dark."[44]

Contrary to the atheists, we believe all human beings have an immortal soul which leaves the body at death, going before God in what is called the "particular judgement". If our life has been primarily for God, through his mercy, we may pass through a time of purification, and then enter fully into the experience of heaven. Heaven is communion with God, beholding the very essence of God, Father, Son and Holy Spirit, and being drawn into this infinite abyss of divine love. The *Catholic Catechism* describes this state succinctly:

This perfect life with the Most Holy Trinity – communion of life and love with the Trinity, with the Virgin Mary, the angels and all the blessed – is called 'heaven'. Heaven is the ultimate end and fulfillment of the deepest human longings, the state of supreme, definitive happiness.[45]

St Paul, while in prison in Philippi, struggled within himself whether it would be better to be martyred immediately or to continue with his mission here on earth: "I do not know what I should choose. I am caught in this dilemma. I want to be gone and be with Christ, which would be very much the better, but for me to stay alive in this body is a more urgent need for your sake" (Phil 1:23-24). He obviously expected that to die meant to be immediately "with Christ". Those who enter heaven live fully "in Christ". Jesus promised this to his apostles at the Last Supper. Knowing he was leaving them, he gave words of encouragement that are popularly used in funeral liturgies, "I am going to prepare a place for you, and after I have gone and prepared you a place, I shall return to take you with me; so that where I am you may be too" (Jn 14:2-3). Likewise in the parable of the talents when Jesus is affirming those who were genuinely responsible in their discipleship, they hear the words, "well done, good and faithful servant… enter into the joy of your Master" (Mt 25:21).

An escapist mentality?

We need to be careful in promoting heaven as a future state of happiness that we do not foster an escapist mentality. Occasionally we can find this in the hearts of Christians. Things are too hard here, so let's put all our focus on the "pie in the sky when we die". That attitude would be a misuse of the idea of heaven. We don't want to be chasing a futuristic kingdom promised by the Lord and avoid the real challenges of our earthly journey. Nevertheless, we would be crazy to ignore that our deepest yearning is for union with God, which ultimately is heaven. This is our destiny. If we aren't focused on our proper end, we will be wandering like nomads on earth. We will be lost in a contemporary wilderness without meaning or purpose, enslaved to momentary passions and desires, bereft of the knowledge of the true dignity bestowed on human beings by God. We are made for heaven. We need to enflame this longing more and more.

Stoking the desire for heaven, rather than opting out of this world's concerns, immerses us even more deeply in the world, since that is the heart of God. There is no other way to God, and ultimately to heaven, except through the nitty-gritty of our present condition and responding to the exigencies of our earthly life right now. Ultimately, the journey into heaven is about loving God with our whole heart, mind and soul, and loving others as oneself. For most of us this is not in the seclusion of a monastery, and for all of us, no matter what our state of life, it will be a very down to earth experience, rather than "living in the clouds" indifferent to the plight of our contemporaries in today's world. The ultimate test of our lives will be how we have loved here on earth in a practical way.

Coming home

One way of thinking about death and entry into heaven is as a "home-coming", like none other; the ultimate entry into the Father's house forever. Death will take us into the darkness of Jesus on the Cross when his soul felt like he was losing his Father, but he trusted all the same in the Father's faithfulness. Jesus plunged into the lostness of humanity, for our sake, only to be lifted out of this dark hole by the Father, who summonsed him in resurrection with words such as, "Come then, my love, my lovely one come!" (Song of Songs 2:13) Our entry into heaven has been opened up by Jesus' resurrection. Even though our body will not catch up until the Last Day, our very self enters into glory with the Father. Resurrection day was the Father's response to Jesus' sacrifice; the day of reunion, when the Father welcomed his Son home. As Cantalamessa puts it, "The resurrection is first of all a gift of the Father to his beloved Son in whom he is well pleased. It was his embrace after the atrocious separation of the Cross, an act of infinite fatherly tenderness".[46] Jesus assured his apostles he was returning to the Father's house to prepare a place for each of us. There will come a time when we will be invited to take our place there, which he has prepared for us (Jn 14:2).

I was touched by a story I heard about a member of the only "leper colony" in the United States which finally closed in 2015.[47] In Carville Louisiana this home for victims of Hansen's disease was for those who were receiving continuing treatment. Yolanda, who was thirty-seven years old had contracted the disease five years previously. It had ravaged her body, which previously had been naturally very beautiful. Her husband was an alcoholic and had abandoned her because of the social stigma and had demanded their two boys stay away. Yolanda was not responding to treatment and was dying, an abandoned and forsaken woman. When she received the anointing of the sick, her face lit up as if the sun was shining on her. Her friend said, "Yolanda, you appear to be happy". With her slight Mexican-American accent she said, "Oh yes, I am so happy". When asked about the source of her happiness she said, "The Father of Jesus just told me that He would take me home today". After a lengthy pause her friend asked what the Father of Jesus had said. Yolanda replied she heard the words: "Come now, my love. My lovely one come".

Apparently, Yolanda had little knowledge of Scripture, but in this moment of extremity she heard the Father calling her home in these beautiful words spoken to the beloved in the Song of Songs (2:13-14). She heard the voice of the Father calling her out of "the cleft of the rock in which she had hidden" due to shame and guilt, not feeling capable of showing her face. She heard the Father call her, "show me your face, let me hear your voice, for your voice is sweet and your face is beautiful". I suspect with many of us we will feel similarly as we come face to face with our Beloved in death. We will feel the shame and guilt of our poor lives, but these words from the Father may well be what we will hear at that moment of extremity. The Father longs to bring us to himself. Let's trust ourselves into his loving hands and seek to remove from our lives anything that would prevent us being able to respond to his invitation to eternal bliss. We will surely feel inadequate to enter into glory, but we can throw ourselves totally upon his heart of infinite mercy.

This mystery of being in total union with Christ and participating in the life of the Trinity forever is beyond description. As I have mentioned, Scripture uses the image of the Father's house. But also, images of life, light, peace, wedding feast, wine of the kingdom, the heavenly Jerusalem, and paradise. These images help us increase our desire for the ultimate happiness of heaven, but fail to give us a truly vivid description of what heaven is like. We are left largely in ignorance, but that should not surprise us. Heaven involves being plunged forever into the mystery of God's infinite love. Mystics down through the ages have insisted that the more we come to know about God the more we discover we don't know. We live by faith in this earthly pilgrimage, and while faith gives a light of illumination it also leaves us in profound darkness as we come into fuller knowledge of God. Paul tells us, "Eye has not seen, nor ear heard, nor heart of man conceived what God has prepared for those who love him" (1Cor 2:9). This way of "not knowing" in our earthly journey is all we are capable of attaining. As Paul exclaims: "How rich are the depths of God! How deep his wisdom and knowledge! How unsearchable are his judgements, how inscrutable his ways! Who would ever know the mind of the Lord? Who could ever be his counsellor?" (Rom 11: 33-34)

Beholding the essence of God

The saints who have been granted profound experiences of God attest to the impossibility of explaining such an encounter. These foretastes of the divine mystery leave them speechless. God is ultimately incomprehensible and beyond our capacity to know him, except indirectly, while on this earthy pilgrimage. Catherine of Siena, after being granted visions, could not describe what she experienced to Raymond of Capua, her spiritual director. All she could say is, "I have seen the hidden things of God". St Paul was granted "visions and revelations from the Lord", not only on the Damascus road, but also later in his journey. Reluctantly, almost in a moment of weakness he admits to the Corinthians, "I know a man in Christ who, fourteen years ago, was caught up – whether still in the body or out of the body, I do not know; God knows – right into the third heaven. I do not know, however, that this same person – whether in the body or out of the body, I do not know; God knows – was caught up into paradise and heard things which must not and cannot be put into human language" (2 Cor 12:1-4). Thomas Aquinas, towards the end of his life had such a profound encounter with Christ in the Eucharist that he decided to write no more. Even though his writings remain today fundamental texts for the church's teaching, his direct experience of Christ was too overwhelming. When his secretary pressed him to explain, he replied, "All I have written seems to be nothing but straw". The Lord brought him to silence, in preparation for his entry into heaven.

Those in heaven are no longer moving in the mode of faith, which is characteristic of our journey on earth. Faith has now been superseded. The glorified move by sight. The Church has always maintained that in heaven we will *see God as he really is*. While on our earthly pilgrimage we may be gifted with ecstatic visions of God, but these are still nothing compared to what is granted in heaven. God opens up his infinite mystery of love to those in heaven, so they are given the capacity to contemplate him "immediately" i.e., without any mediation. This is a qualitatively different experience than anything else: infinitely more wonderful than the way even the most blessed mystics experience him on this earthly journey. The veil is drawn back, and we behold "the essence of God". Paul, writing to the Corinthians, after extolling the primacy of love, proclaims that love does not come to an end. Love is brought to perfection in heaven. Knowledge and prophecy will pass away, but love will remain. He says, "When I was a child, I used to talk like a child, and think like a child, and argue like a child, but now I am a man, all childish ways are put behind me". With this analogy in mind, he refers to the future yet to come, "Now we are seeing a dim reflection in a mirror; but then we shall be seeing face to face. The knowledge that I have now is imperfect; but then I shall know as fully as I am known" (1 Cor 13:11-12).

While we keep pushing ahead on our earthly journey, we are meant to uncover increasingly our in-built deep desire for God. The psalmist prays, "Of you my heart has spoken: 'Seek his face'. It is your face, O Lord, that I seek; hide not your face" (Ps 27:8-9). This aspiration is written deeply in our hearts, longing for the ultimate encounter with God. What we experience now is very real, but still "as through a glass darkly". Yet, we should not underestimate the extraordinary grace given to us when we allow the Holy Spirit to light up our hearts and awaken us to a deep hunger for God. Already, through grace, because of our baptism, we have been brought into the life of the Trinity. Already a light shines in our hearts through faith. Through the action of the Spirit within us, Paul says, we are "being changed into the likeness of Christ from one degree of glory to the next. This is the work of the Lord who is Spirit" (2 Cor 4:18). Already we have a taste of heaven. As Elizabeth of the Trinity reminds us, heaven is within us already, to the extent that we open ourselves to his presence. Paul continues, "It is the same God who said, 'Let there be light shining in the darkness', who has shone in our minds to radiate the light of the knowledge of God's glory, the glory shining on the face of Christ" (2 Cor 4:6).

Experience of heaven begins now

Already by grace we experience a foretaste of heaven, and encounter the face of Christ within us. Because of the sanctifying grace of baptism, eternal life begins now. This spurs us forward to the fullness of what is yet to come. There is a beautiful text in John's first letter which sums up this teaching:

> Think of the love that the Father has lavished on us by letting us be called God's children; and that is what we are … My dear people, we are already the children of God, but what we are to be in the future has not yet been revealed; all we know is, that when it is revealed we shall be like him because we shall see him as he really is. Surely everyone who entertains this hope must purify himself, must try to be as pure as Christ (1 Jn 3:1-3).

Already we share in God's life; already by his Spirit within us we are children of God, heirs of the Kingdom to come. His indwelling presence is real, bringing us into communion with him. This is the beginning of what we will know in heaven. Elizabeth of the Trinity asserts with the confidence and simplicity of the saints: "It seems to me that I have found my Heaven on earth, because my Heaven is God, and God is in my soul. The day I understood that, everything became clear to me."[48]

While now our experience of heaven is limited, when through death we come into the Father's house we shall "see him as he really is" with no intermediaries, no longer relying on images or our intellect alone. Now the intellect will be flooded with light giving direct apprehension of the inner life of God. The love of God will inflame the will so completely that our whole being will be expanded in love for God and for others like never before. We shall be "like him". How we struggle on this earthly pilgrimage to be like God! How we have fought to overcome the hindrances within us to being transformed into his likeness! Now by the flooding of God's immense love we will be perfected in love. This text from John, cited earlier, refers to the need for purification. No matter how much we have cooperated with God's grace on earth, perfection has probably not been fully achieved. Thus the need for purgatory, which we will discuss further in the next chapter.

Growing in knowledge and love

In heaven we will receive the illumination to understand our earthly life in the light of God's wisdom. Don't you sometimes want answers to the imponderable things that happen, especially the unexpected tragedies, our own failures, and a true perspective on our joyful moments? All will be revealed. Much of what we have experienced within God's providence has been so mysterious, and beyond explanation. We will only understand fully from the perspective of heaven. We will also come to know the lives of others more completely, beyond what is possible now. But all will be revealed in an ennobling way where there will be no shame or disgrace, only God's understanding, wisdom, mercy and love. Relationships will be totally open and vulnerable, perfected in love. But the most exciting and joyful reality will be forever deepening in our knowledge and love for God. Our mind and our will shall not be static, fixed in eternal gaze upon God, as if we just keep focusing on the same reality for eternity. Rather we will be fully human and fully alive, which means we will be forever exploring more deeply the mystery of God. Forever overwhelmed by the beauty of God, the mind will be forever deepening in the truth of God, and the will shall be forever deepening in love.

I once was speaking to a prayer meeting about worship. I was encouraging the group to allow the Holy Spirit to lift their hearts in praise of God. I was urging them not to be afraid to speak out their praises and to sing in joyful exaltation of God. We praise him because he is worthy of praise; we worship him for his goodness, kindness, mercy and love. We adore him, and surrender all we are to him. Then I mentioned to them we will be doing this forever in heaven, because this is the highest function of the human being. A young lad in the front was startled, and blurted out, "You mean for eternity! How boring!" No doubt he was voicing the unexpressed reluctance of others in the group as well. For myself also, due to our present fleshy condition it is difficult to imagine being caught up in God forever! Surely, I would want to have a break for a coffee! Our limited images and our contemporary experience make it almost impossible to think of heaven. This should not cause us dismay. The immensity of God and his utter incomprehensibility leaves us, as Paul says, "looking through a glass darkly". However, the best sense we can get of heaven is to remember the moments of deep joy in the Lord, the moments when we were wrapped up in worship of him, or moments when we felt so lifted when we extended ourselves in love of another, especially one in great need. Then extrapolate that joy, multiplying it a billion times, and we may gain some hint of heavenly glory.

Blessed in heaven for us

If heaven is the total immersion into the love of God, then surely it cannot be insulated in some way from all those we have left behind on earth. The blessed in heaven enter into communion with God, and this means also a deeper communion with one another. In Christ they will share in his love for us; they will be in communion with us on our earthly pilgrimage. They will know all about us. They will not be impassive towards our plight. They will have reached the pinnacle of love, joined perfectly in the saving love of God for all people. As we explained in the last chapter, they will still be deeply involved with us who remain on the earthly pilgrimage. Together we make up the communion of saints. They will know our problems and have a deep compassion for our plight. They will not be indifferent but will be moved by our needs since they share in the loving heart of God. They will be keen to facilitate the voyage of their friends and relatives, as well as everyone else who calls on them. They will be waiting for us to join them and will be fully concerned for us. So, it is highly advantageous for us to call on the help of the saints, both those officially recognised and those others who are not. The only difference is that we cannot develop public devotions to those who are not beatified, since as yet it is not certain they have reached heaven.

Every member of the pilgrim Church on earth is bound to all the others in a profound way. This bond is so strong that it cannot be broken even by death. In Christ we can never be separated from those whom we love. So, in heaven, while the manner of being together has changed, the bond in Christ cannot be broken.[49] As I mentioned above this means those who have gone before us to heaven will have a particular concern for our welfare, and we can beg for their help. In the Catholic church, we have never been shy about relating with our friends in heaven and calling upon them for help at decisive moments in life. However, we give more credence to those who have been beatified, since we can be sure they are in heaven and guaranteed of their help. We beg for their intercession. The favours they grant are not given from them but from the Lord. Because they live in the Lord most intimately their intercession is powerful. We can have our special patrons, or our chosen friends amongst the beatified. When we turn to them for help, we know because they are close to us they will intercede for us. Maybe a parish community dedicated to a particular saint, or a religious community with its founder, or maybe the baptismal or confirmation name one bears, or maybe just a saint you have "adopted", whatever the origin of the devotion, we know that their assistance is real.

Of all the saints the most powerful in intercession is the Blessed Virgin Mary. Our Blessed Mother's intercession is *special, extraordinary and universal*.[50] It is *special* because her intimacy with Christ is unique. It is *extraordinary* since she is "full of grace", surrendered totally to the will of God, and has become for all people their "mother in the order of grace". Her intercession is unique because of the way she was chosen to cooperate with God's plan for the salvation of the world. She continues this work as a servant in heaven. Mary's intercession is *universal* in extent, because the work of redemption embraces the whole of humanity, and she was at the heart of God's plan for redeeming the whole world. Mary is Queen of heaven. Just as the queen mothers in the Old Testament had persuasive power over their kingly sons, so does our Blessed Mother have unique influence in obtaining blessings for us through her Son, the King of kings. The story of the wedding feast at Cana in Galilee reveals this so poignantly. Mary brings to him our deepest needs, "They have no wine". Nothing is attained except through the one Mediator, Jesus, our Saviour, but the mystery of our communion with the saints and especially with our Blessed Mother, gives us great confidence in their intercession on our behalf.

5
PURGATORY

Purgatory is not part of the doctrine of hell. Those enduring purgatory are already entering into full union with God. Their suffering is qualitatively different from that of the damned. They know they have attained salvation. They are on their way to heaven. So, an authentic understanding of purgatory is derived from the doctrine of heaven. Immediately after death souls encounter Christ's merciful judgement. If they are called to enter heaven, they may need to go through purgatory, but they will still be full of joy and hope because their eternal end is established. They are already falling into the ultimate experience of God's love. His love is likened to fire. As we read in the Song of Songs: "Love is a flash of fire from the heart of God, a fire which no torrents can quench and no floods drown." (Song 8:6). They are flooded with the Holy Spirit who is the fire of God's love cleansing and purifying them.

Purgatory is not a place of torture, but a state of purgation, which is necessary as we enter into the holiness of God. God is holy and cannot abide with sin. When we encounter the living God we become aware of the depth of our disfigurement and proneness to evil, and realise our nothingness and total dependence upon him. All the arrogance of the human heart becomes obvious. While we may not be guilty of serious sin we will see ever more clearly the reality of our compromise and our propensity to sin. As Hebrews tells us, "It is a fearful thing to fall into the hands of the living God" (Heb 10:31)

Purification by fire

Encounter with God confronts us with our sinfulness. When Isaiah was overwhelmed by the presence of the God in the Temple, he saw the Lord seated on a high throne, surrounded by seraphs, crying out, "Holy, Holy, Holy is the Lord of hosts. His glory fills the whole earth". The experience of the holiness of God was so overwhelming that he could feel his utter sinfulness: "What a wretched state I am in! I am lost, for I am a man of unclean lips and I live amongst a people of unclean lips, and my eyes have looked at the King, the Lord of hosts" (Is 6:1-6). He had to be purified. One of the seraphs brought a live coal which he had taken from the altar with a pair of tongs. He touched the mouth of Isaiah, saying "See now, this has touched your lips, your sin is taken away, your iniquity purged". This is the dynamic of purgatory. We are falling into the hands of the living God, who is love. His love must purify us. We are not capable of doing the necessary purging. Only God, who is all holy, can do this for us. Surely it is a painful process, but it is liberating. We will joyfully accept this purgation, and hold great hope in our hearts, because we are encountering God and allowing his love to transform us as only he can do.

Purgatory does not involve a physical burning. Yet the burning is real and painful, since it is a purification of the soul. This is the ultimate healing that we need, which must happen if it has not already occurred before death. Bad habits must be overcome, resentments relinquished, ignorance corrected, deeply rooted bitterness and even hatred extinguished. The fire of God's love sears deeply into those parts of our being as yet not fully given to God. In the lives of saints who experience mystical union with God we get a glimpse of what purgatory is like. John of the Cross has described the agonising purifications in the spirit of a person seeking union with God. He speaks of "a living flame of love that tenderly wounds my soul in its deepest centre".[51] Maybe his description of transformation which the Spirit brings to the soul in the passive night is the closest we can come to understanding the dynamic of purgatory:

> This dark night is an inflow of God into the soul, which purges it of its habitual ignorance and imperfections, natural and spiritual…..Through this contemplation, God teaches the soul secretly and instructs it in the perfections of love without its doing anything, nor understanding how this happens … there are two reasons why this divine wisdom is not only night and darkness for the soul, but also affliction and torment. First, because of the height of the divine wisdom which exceeds the capacity of the soul. Second, because of the soul's baseness and impurity; and on this account it is painful, afflictive, and also dark for the soul.[52]

The purification that we are describing here does not happen through some thing, such as weapons of punishment or whatever. It is the Lord himself who is the judging fire which transforms us and conforms us to his own glorified body. Nothing is applied to us from outside as it were. Instead we experience interior transformation through the power of the Lord himself, "whose burning flame cuts free our closed-off heart, melting it, and pouring into it a new mould to make it fit for the living organism of his body".[53] Pope Benedict XVI, before becoming Pope, taught:

> Purgatory is not, as Tertullian thought, some kind of supra-worldly concentration camp where man is forced to undergo punishment in a more or less arbitrary fashion. Rather it is the inwardly necessary process of transformation in which a person becomes capable of Christ, capable of God and thus capable of unity with the whole communion of saints.[54]

Our need for purgation

Our own self-knowledge should convince us fairly quickly of the need for such a purgation. Who could in their right mind at this point in their earthly journey think they are totally in union with God, akin to heaven? Except for relatively few who may have attained a high state of mystical union with God, most of us on this earthly pilgrimage have not yet yielded to the penetration of the Holy Spirit's transforming work to the extent that we are fully ready for heaven. We all have been redeemed by the precious blood of Jesus, and many are on a true journey of discipleship, but who could claim our encounter with the Lord has already dealt fully with the fundamental disorders of the human heart and made us fully holy in him? This ultimate encounter with Christ through death and immediate judgement sets off a process of finishing the work already begun. Purgatory is the fire of God's love which "burns away our dross and re-forms us to be vessels of eternal joy".[55] On the one hand there is this painful fire of love which purges all selfishness still deep within the heart and opens the heart to love as never before, but on the other hand the heart is full of joy both in already knowing the love of God which is beyond all knowledge and in anticipation of perfection in heaven.

In the light of God's penetrating love, we will become more intensely aware of the darkness within ourselves. We will see our own arrogant ingratitude, gross pride and self-centredness, and spirit of independence before the humble, self-sacrificing love of God, Father, Son and Holy Spirit. In this earthly life we find it difficult to really surrender to the Lord, to let him have control of our lives, to allow him to do the deeper surgery in the heart that needs to happen. Now in the ultimate moment of truth we will find ourselves lacking mercy, love and justice. We will need to bring what could be rightly called punishment upon ourselves. We will see more clearly than ever our misguided priorities and how we have neglected the poor and been indifferent to their needs. We will be filled with sorrow for our failings in loving God and loving others. Now will not be a time for repentance, since there is no repentance after death, but simply to endure the consequences of our selfish choices and misdeeds, knowing like never before, with clear illumination of soul, our utter need for the transforming power of God.

Deepening of our life of holiness

During our earthly journey many of us have experienced a new outpouring of the fire of the Holy Spirit, granting a new capacity to love others, a deeper level of compunction, and a deep gratitude overflowing into praise for the immense love of God. How much more will we experience this in purgatory! It will be an ever-deeper experience of the saving love of God revealed in Jesus Christ and flowing into our hearts by the Holy Spirit, which will do the necessary finishing work within us. Piet Fransen describes this purifying love of God:

> It is love that causes our greatest pain, pain far greater than any we can bear on earth. It scorches in us all the remnants of our self-love, ingratitude and refusal. But at the same time it penetrates us totally, which is why purgatory is also a joy more intense than anything we can experience on earth.[56]

Many commentators down through the centuries have drawn upon St. Paul's witness to help bolster the concept of purgatory. Paul uses the image of a building. He speaks of how he has laid good foundations when preaching to the Corinthians. Now someone else, Apollos, is building on these foundations. But he is quick to say the foundation of the work is really Christ, and no one can change that. He continues:

> On this foundation you can build in gold, silver and jewels, or in wood, grass and straw, but whatever the material, the work of each builder is going to be clearly revealed when the day comes. That day will begin with fire, and the fire will test the quality of each man's work...if his building is burnt down, he will be the loser, and though he is saved himself, it will be as one who has gone through fire (1 Cor 3:10-15).

This text is useful even though its original context is in relation to the work of preaching and teaching. Paul is comparing his foundational preaching to that of Apollos who built on his original proclamation of the gospel. The value of each person's work will be brought to light on the day of judgement. But the image of fire can be extended to refer not only to what apostolic works we manage to achieve, but also to our own personal transformation in holiness. We must be hopeful that even though we have had many failures and it may seem that the "building" has been in vain, we can still be saved by the mercy of God, but "as one who has gone through fire"!

Praying for those in purgatory

Those still on their earthly pilgrimage can help those in purgatory by their prayers. We are told in Scripture, "It is a holy and wholesome thought to pray for the dead that they may be loosed from their sins" (2 Mac. 12:45-46). We know that from earliest times Christians prayed for their dead as an act of solidarity and charity, understanding that their prayers would be effective in helping "the holy souls". This was a universal practice, found in the writings of the early Fathers, both from the East and West, such as Tertullian, Origen, Cyprian, Ambrose, Augustine, Basil, Gregory of Nazianzus, Gregory of Nyssa and John Chrysostom. Inscriptions on tombstones from earliest times attest to the strong belief that prayers for the dead would be effective. When people were dying, they also begged for prayers that God may bring them eternal rest. In the early Fathers it seems that they only expected very few to have full entry to heaven immediately. For most people they expected a need for a purifying by fire.

As Catholics it comes almost naturally for us to pray for the dead. We include prayers for the departed in every Mass, and at funeral Masses or liturgies of remembrance we explicitly commend to the Lord those who have died. I have included an appendix at the end of this book explaining some of the technical language the Church uses in regard to praying for those in purgatory, including the doctrine on indulgences. Most importantly, praying for those in purgatory is an act of charity, since we know our prayers can be effective in helping them attain the fullness of God.

6
HELL

Today in theological circles there is an unhealthy trend toward the view that ultimately all people will be saved due to the mercy of God. Preachers don't actually deny the existence of hell, but simply ignore it, putting all their emphasis on how Jesus offers fullness of life now. Given the modern mentality which is primarily about "what is in it for me now", I can see good reasons for the initial pitch of evangelising preaching to emphasise the love and mercy of God. In fact, we should never diverge from God's mercy. But within this ambit of God's love people need to be convinced also of the truth of hell. The way this is included in preaching requires much sensitivity. Using hell to frighten people into accepting Christ does not yield good fruit. I prefer to win souls through love rather than through fear. Even if they are won to the Church in some way through fear, they will probably bear a warped view of the gospel of Christ.

Once when we were doing some street preaching in Canberra, we had set up a large cross and an icon of Our Lady to make sure people knew we were Catholic. As usual we would sing some attractive hymns and then for three minutes or so one of the brothers would take his turn proclaiming God's love for all people, while the other brothers would gently approach passers-by to engage them in friendly conversation. But to our dismay, on this particular day, another Christian group arrived in the same square and began preaching a message of condemnation, warning people that they are all on the slippery road to hell and they had better repent before it is too late. Rather than get into a confrontation, we quietly collected our gear and packed up for the day. Their negative message was undermining our more friendly approach. Like the other group we had a keen desire to win people for Jesus, but we seek to win by attraction not by polemics.

This episode reminded me of my early years as an altar boy in a country town in NSW. The annual retreat conducted by the missionary priest always drew a crowd. The church would be full each night for a whole week. The most memorable night was always the one dedicated to the preaching on eternal destiny. The lights were lowered for dramatic effect. Then the preacher in flowing robes appeared out of the gloom, a single spotlight came upon him. With a sonorous voice he shouted one word, "HELL!" And then with a flourish he repeated the warning ever more dramatically. The whole congregation shivered in fear. Then for forty minutes or more he had us dangling by a thread over the fires of hell. Needless to say, when he had finished his act, long lines of parishioners lined up at the confessional. As a young lad I was very impressed with the drama, but I was probably a little too young to be conscience-stricken like the adults. Maybe it's not fair to make too harsh an assessment of such missionary tactics. However, this style of preaching bred into the people an image of God as a punitive figure, not true to the Father revealed by Jesus. Alfonsus Liguori, the founder of the Redemptorists, a well-known missionary congregation, had this to say about the matter:

Conversions merely from terror do not last – these motives are soon forgotten. But whoever is converted through consideration of the love of Jesus Christ, their conversion is more genuine and lasting. Fear will not achieve what love can achieve. Sometimes a sermon which causes fear can be dismissed with a shrug of the shoulder but one spark of the love of God is sufficient to burn up everything else. [57]

Is hell real?

We live in a culture which no longer believes in hell. We are a long way from the mediaeval times when the whole world-view of men and women involved heaven, hell, and purgatory as taken-for- granted realities. In Church circles today hell has largely disappeared from the radar. It rarely gets a mention, other than in some jest regarding demons, which also have become, in the minds of many, the imaginary stuff of folk tales. Yet hell remains firmly part of the Church's teaching. The *Catholic Catechism* says quite clearly:

> To die in mortal sin without repenting and accepting God's merciful love means remaining separated from him for ever by our own free choice. This state of definitive self-exclusion from communion with God and the blessed is called "hell".[58]

Jesus warns about the possibility of going to hell when we die. He often refers to Gehenna, or the "unquenchable fire". The image is taken from the valley of Hinnom which was the garbage dump for the city of Jerusalem. It was burning day and night. Gehenna became the metaphorical name for hell, an underground region of fire where the damned are punished after death. This is in contrast to the prospect of paradise, an entry into eternal bliss. For example, the parable of the wheat and the darnel : "The Son of Man will send his angels and they will gather out of his kingdom all things that provoke offences and all who do evil, and throw them in the blazing furnace, where there will be weeping and grinding of teeth" (Mt 13:41-42). And to those who refused to love the least in the world the King will say on judgment day, "Go away from me with your curse upon you, to the eternal fire prepared for the devil and his angels. For I was hungry and you never gave me food, I was thirsty and you never gave me anything to drink; I was a stranger and you never made me welcome, naked and you never clothed me, sick and in prison and you never visited me" (Mt 25: 41-43).

Immediate Punishment

We find that the Scriptures also testify to the possibility of an immediate entry into hell after death. Jesus tells the fate of the rich man who ignored Lazarus suffering at his door. When the poor man died, he was carried into the bosom of Abraham. The rich man went to torment in Hades. The rich man begs for a drop of water to be brought to his parched tongue. Abraham replies:

> "My son, remember that during your life good things came your way, just as bad things came the way of Lazarus. Now he is being comforted while you are in agony. But that is not all: between us and you a great gulf has been fixed, to stop anyone, if he wanted to, crossing from our side to yours, and to stop anyone crossing from your side to ours" (Lk 16:23-26).

This text refers to Hades, the Greek translation of the Hebrew Sheol, which was commonly understood to be where people went immediately after death. It had an upper part which was akin to paradise. But the lower part was a place of suffering and punishment for those who have been evil. This parable makes it clear that in Jesus' mind the separation of the good and evil was irrevocable. We remember also the so called "good thief" who prayed "Jesus, remember me when you come into your kingdom" and Jesus replied, "This day you will be with me in paradise". Immediately after death one goes either to eternal punishment or to eternal bliss.

There are many other texts in the gospels alluding to the possibility of eternal punishment. As the Vatican II document *Lumen Gentium* says:

> Since we know neither the day nor the hour, we should follow the advice of the Lord and watch constantly so that when the single course of our earthly life is completed, we may merit to enter with him into the marriage feast and be numbered among the blessed, and not, like the wicked and slothful servants, be ordered to depart into the eternal fire, into the outer darkness where "men will weep and gnash their teeth"(cf. Mt 22:13).[59]

Many mystics have received revelations of the horror of hell. St Faustina Kowalska was given a vision of the tortures of hell, only so she could proclaim more intensely the great mercy of God for those who turn to him. While we need not linger over the various images given her of the agony of the damned, I found her summary statement disturbing, and worth repeating here. She writes, "What I have written is but a pale shadow of the things I saw. But I noticed one thing: that most of the souls there are those who disbelieved that there is a hell".[60] Many Catholics would also be aware of the vision of hell given to the children at Fatima, and how Our Lady gave them a prayer which we all pray at the end of each decade of the Rosary, "O my Jesus, forgive us our sins, save us from the fires of hell. Bring all souls to heaven, especially who most need your mercy".

Pope Francis in a morning homily encouraged his listeners not to be frightened of hell, but he warned, "It is the truth. If you don't take care of your heart and always live far away from the Lord, perhaps there is the danger of continuing in this way, far away from the Lord for eternity!"[61] The Catechism says, "The chief punishment of hell is eternal separation from God, in whom alone man can possess the life of happiness he was created and for which he longs."[62] Hell is a state of utter desolation, a lonely place, which Dante in his Inferno likens to a lake of ice, a place of darkness, frozen in despair.[63]

Sr Lucia, one of the visionaries at Fatima, who were given a vision of hell, noted that while those in hell were suffering intense physical pain, the deepest agony was that of despair. It means being alone, separated from God and humanity, away forever from all that is true, good and beautiful.

In a chilling rebuke of the bosses of the Mafia in Italy, Pope Francis did not mince words. He appeals to them to change their ways before it is too late.

> We are praying for you. Convert, I ask it on my knees; it is for your own good. This life you are living now, it won't bring you pleasure, it won't give you joy, it won't

bring you happiness. The power, the money, that you possess now from so many dirty transactions, from so many mafia crimes, is blood-stained money, it is power soaked in blood, and you cannot take it with you to the next life. Convert, there is still time, so that you don't end up in hell. That is what awaits you if you continue on this path.[64]

Why does hell exist?

How can we explain the existence of hell? There seems to be two important points to make. Firstly, hell exists because of free will given us by God. Secondly, as a corollary of the first reason, hell exists because of the holiness of God. God does not send anyone to hell. Rather people choose to go to hell rather than live under God's will. C.S. Lewis puts the matter very clearly:

> There are only two kinds of people in the end: those who say to God, 'Thy will be done', and those to whom God says, in the end, 'Thy will be done'. All who are in hell choose to be there. Without that self-choice there could be no hell. No soul that seriously and constantly desires joy will ever miss it. Those who seek find, to those who knock, it is opened.[65]

The reality is that human beings can rebel from God in such a way that is irrevocable. The nature of the so-called "great divorce" between heaven and hell, as described by Lewis, comes down to the inherent resistance in human beings to submit to God's ways:

> "Milton was right", said my Teacher, "the choice of every lost soul can be expressed in the words, 'Better to reign in Hell than to serve in Heaven'." There is always something they insist on keeping, even at the price of misery. There

is always something they prefer to joy – that is to reality …In adult life it has a hundred fine names – Achilles wrath … Revenge and injured merit and self-respect and tragic greatness and proper pride.[66]

I want to underline this notion of what the Catechism calls "self-exclusion" and Lewis calls "self-choice". Bernard of Clairvaux says of those in hell, "they prefer to be unhappy in their own sovereignty rather than be happy in submission".[67] In choosing absolute autonomy the creature is aware of the unhappiness and darkness involved, but is willing to pay this price. Rather reign in hell than serve in heaven! It is stuff that puts a shiver down your spine. The eternity of hell does not depend on God, who is always ready to forgive, but on the person who does not want to be forgiven. If God did forgive without their consent, the damned would accuse God of not respecting their freedom. G.K. Chesterton made the telling comment, "Hell is God's great compliment to the reality of human freedom and the dignity of human choice". C.S. Lewis backs this up, "Hell is the greatest monument to human freedom".

Possible deception

We should not underestimate the deceptive power of Satan who tempts people today as he did in the Garden of Eden. Those who deny the existence of hell may well be pawns of Satan. In today's world many are succumbing to the lie that they can construct a "rebirth" of themselves through self-will, becoming absolute master of oneself, with unlimited pride and power, being king of my own world. They can easily become pawns of Satan, living under the ultimate deception of what St Paul calls "impiety", the refusal to worship God (Rom 1:21). This trend sets up an antithesis to the genuine "rebirth" that comes to the human being through the Holy Spirit when we submit our wills in obedience to God. In reality Satan has no power, but he can deceive and keep people in bondage. He exists and persists through deception. Unfortunately, it is possible that some can be so deceived that they buy into this ruse irrevocably. They no longer want any way back. They prefer the pain of hell to the love of God. They cannot stand God's presence. He does not reject them. They reject him. If they cannot endure his presence, then God consistently gives them the freedom to condemn themselves to eternal loss. The Lord says, in a colloquial way, something like this: "I will not force you to accept my love. If you resist, I will not compel you. There will come a day of reckoning. If you don't want what I am offering, you will not be able to endure my presence. You will shut yourself out from my presence."

There is a second subsidiary reason for the existence of hell. This comes from the very nature of God, who is all holy. Heaven, as we have seen, is the last end of those who have surrendered to the holiness of God. They have deeply desired God so much that they have allowed him to purify them both on earth and through purgatory, so they can live fully in his presence. The reality is that God's holiness and human sin are objectively incompatible. This is what we mean by the "wrath of God". This scriptural phrase does not mean emotional anger, but simply that God is holy and sin is incompatible with his nature. Those who are so self-enclosed in their own self-invention and unwilling to succumb to the purifying work of God cannot abide in God. They must be separated from him. God cannot compromise who he is. He cannot accommodate the sin of which they are unwilling to repent. An unbridgeable gap must exist between them. But as we have insisted, this gap is not caused by God but by the inhabitants of hell. Those in hell do not have the capacity for heaven; their self-chosen state excludes them from the holiness of God.

Will all be saved?

The question arises whether God will ultimately bring everything together in heaven. Will everyone be ultimately saved? Some would argue that it contradicts the infinite mercy of God if the condemned will be left in hell for eternity. Wouldn't his universal desire to save all men and women win out in the end? This doctrine arose in the early church with Origen and other church fathers, including Gregory of Nyssa, Theodore of Mopsuestia, and Evagrius Ponticus. It took the name *apokatastasis*, meaning "restoration". But the broad Tradition of the Church did not adopt this thinking.

This mistaken notion of an ultimate universal reconciliation has resurfaced in our times through theologians seeking to make sense of the anomaly that an all- good God could possibly be satisfied to see even one of his creatures suffering the torments of hell forever. Hans Urs von Balthasar, one of the most prominent Catholic theologians of the 20th century, struggled with this question. While not crossing over into heresy he held a fine line. On the one hand he acknowledged the existence of hell, but on the other hand doubted it has ever been populated, or at least that we can hope that the time will come when all will be saved.

Balthasar's concerns, expressed in a book entitled *Dare We Hope That All Men Be Saved?*[68] are primarily around the truth that God's perfect love was expressed when Christ died to save all human beings. Surely God intended his saving work to be totally effective. Is it possible for the obstinacy of human will to ultimately withstand the winning influence of God's merciful love? How could we imagine God being unmoved and callous about the suffering of the damned in hell for eternity? Balthasar emphasises that Christ descended into the emptiness and lostness of hell on Easter Saturday to make it possible for all to be saved. This objective act of redemption was enough for all to find salvation. In addition to this, how can we imagine the saints in heaven not being affected by the lot of their loved ones enduring the fires of hell forever? Balthasar recognises the reality of human freedom but hopes that God's love will eventually conquer human obstinacy and, in the end, all will be brought to salvation. His bottom line is that it is only reasonable to hope that all will be saved.

To back up his "hope" for the salvation of all, he calls on the testimony of saints who in a moment of holy generosity would rather have lost their own souls than see others fall into the awful abandonment of hell. We remember Paul making that prayer in relation to his Jewish brothers and sisters. He says, "my sorrow is so great, my mental anguish so endless, I would willingly be condemned and be cut off from Christ if it could help my brothers of Israel, my own flesh and blood" (Rom 9:2-3). We see this heart for the lost also in mystics such as Catherine of Siena, who declared that provided she could still love God she would gladly endure hell's torments if all others could be saved. She would make her body a stopper against hell – at the mouth of hell laying out her body "to prevent any souls from entering it". She longed to annihilate hell, "I would love that hell should be wiped out; or at least that no souls should ever go there".[69] These testimonies of the heart of God's love expressed by the saints gives Balthasar conviction that God himself, not only the blessed in heaven, could not be impassive to the plight of those in hell. Balthasar is somewhat cynical of those who are strong proponents of eternal punishment. He sees them as judgemental of the huge numbers plunging into hell, while they always conveniently place themselves amongst the relatively few who are "the saved".

Church's teaching on salvation

An unnuanced interpretation of Balthasar's speculations has become recently quite popular in Catholic circles. This is understandable since the current culture has few openings to the transcendent and quickly dismisses any prospect of hell as a possible outcome for our lives. They do a disservice to Balthasar who Pope John Paul II, after three attempts, finally persuaded to become a Cardinal. Unfortunately, Balthasar died before he could receive the red hat. The late Cardinal Avery Dulles, one of the most prominent ecclesiologists of the 20th century, defended Balthasar's orthodoxy, but reminded us of the Church's clear position:

> The constant teaching of the Catholic Church supports the idea that there are two classes of the saved and the damned. Three General Councils of the Church (Lyons 1, 1245; Lyons II, 1274; and Florence, 1439) and Pope

Benedict XII's bull *Benedictus Deus* (1336) have taught that everyone who dies in a state of mortal sin goes immediately to suffer the eternal punishments of hell. This belief has perdured without question in the Catholic Church to this day, and is repeated almost verbatim in the Catechism of the Catholic Church (CCC, 1022, 1035).[70]

It seems like a fog has settled over the minds and hearts of many in the Church. We are hazy about eternal realities. In the first instance we can ignore the *real possibility* that someone who has been fully incorporated into the Catholic church by baptism, confirmation and Eucharist, and accepts all the Church believes and teaches can actually be eternally lost. The Second Vatican Council stated clearly:

> Even though incorporated into the Church, one who does not however persevere in charity is not saved. He remains indeed in the bosom of the Church, but 'in body' not 'in heart'.[71]

Those who have a universalist position, proposing that in the end all will be saved, often claim their position is endorsed by Vatican II. They look to Chapter 16 of *Lumen Gentium*, the flagship document of the Council on the Church. In this chapter, the Council fathers recognise the possibility of salvation of those who, "through no fault of their own, are ignorant of the gospel and the church, but seek God with a sincere heart". Moved by grace and living according to the dictates of their conscience they may be saved even though they are ignorant of Christ. The fathers of the Council also acknowledged the possibility of salvation for those who, seeking to live a good life, but without any fault of their own "have not yet arrived at explicit knowledge of God".

This teaching is far from a *carte blanche* for salvation for anyone outside the Church. There are many nuances to the teaching which cannot be explained fully here.[72] In no way did the Council intend to suggest all will be saved or that we do not need to preach the gospel. The only sure way of entry into the kingdom of God is through explicit commitment to Christ and entry into baptism and the full life of the Church. While the Church is the normal way in God's plan that people attain salvation, those who are outside the Church may under God's saving grace also be saved.

The universalists, who want to convince us that all will be saved, have two main theories. The first is that at the moment of death we will encounter the immensity of the love of Christ in such a powerful way that we cannot but repent of our sins and choose him forever. An appealing notion, but fictional. Why would God so overwhelm our freedom at the end of our earthly pilgrimage when he has created us free and respected that freedom throughout our pilgrim journey here on earth? The second theory is that the doctrine of Jesus' descent into hell assures us that those who go to hell will ultimately be won over by the love of God. Again, this unreal optimism flies in the face of the full weight of the Church's unbroken Tradition, and the unambiguous, consistent teaching of the Magisterium. There is no possibility of conversion after death.

Decision between two paths

So, understanding clearly that there is a path that leads to salvation and another path that leads to damnation is important for every Catholic. It is also imperative that as Church we don't lose the sharpness of our call to mission; to bring to all people the good news of salvation won in Jesus Christ. If we think everyone will be saved anyway then much of the motivation for preaching the Cross of Jesus has been lost. A saccharine message is not going to ultimately help people align their lives with the kingdom of God and take up the narrow path that leads to salvation. The issue is not whether the possibility of going to hell should be part of our preaching, but rather the way we proclaim this sobering message. I am told that the Cure of Ars who was not one to soften the message, or flavour it with so much sugar that it lost its taste, often preached on hell, but always with tears running down his face as he trembled for those who could possibly make such a horrendous ultimate choice in their lives.

The Scriptural evidence is clear. Jesus' famous declaration of the two paths is unavoidable:

> Enter by the narrow gate, since the road that leads to perdition is wide and spacious, and many take it; but it is a narrow gate and a hard road that leads to life, and only a few find it (Mt 7:13-14).

This text seems to indicate clearly that many are on the road to hell, and relatively few are on the way to heaven. But we need to be careful how we use this text. Unfortunately, in his later writings Augustine proposed that the *"massa damnata"*, the large proportion of people on the earth, ultimately end up in hell. His outlook was quite dark in this regard. This rigorous teaching opened up the way for later Protestant interpreters to develop a "double predestination" theory i.e., there are a few who are predestined to heaven, but most are predestined to hell! This sort of thinking was disastrous for Christianity. Coupled with a theory of the redemption which had God the Father exacting his vengeance on the Son as he hung on the Cross, this doctrine left people with a warped notion of God demanding sacrifice to satiate his anger.[73] Thankfully in current times we proclaim more fully that God is love. In creating every human being his will is for them to be ultimately with him forever in heaven.

It is useless to speculate on the question, "How many will be saved?"[74] There is no answer. We are not meant to ask the question. It sets the mind and heart in a negative direction unintended by Jesus. Rather, we are meant to work tirelessly for the salvation of all, preaching the gospel in season and out of season, never presuming on the Lord's goodness, but also never doubting the immensity of his mercy. When Jesus says that many are taking the way to perdition and only a few are heading towards paradise he is using hyperbolic language customary with Jewish rabbis. This is similar to when Jesus says, "if your right hand causes you to sin, cut it off". He does not mean to literally sever your hand. In other words, too much weight could be given to speculations about the proportions of people going the way of salvation or the way of damnation. This is not for us to know.

Undoubtedly God's will is for all to be saved. But human freedom, a wonderful gift from God, can thwart that purpose. The "two ways" text must be taken with all seriousness. Clearly, it is a call to decision. Cut out other options and choose Christ before it is too late. It is a call to embrace the cross, as Jesus expresses elsewhere, "If anyone wants to be a follower of mine he must take up his cross and follow me. Anyone who wants to gain his life will lose it, but the one who loses his life for my sake and for the sake of gospel will find it" (Mt 16:24-25). There is to be no compromise. You can't have it both ways. It is one or the other. A little later Jesus says, "It is not those who say 'Lord', 'Lord', who will enter the kingdom of heaven, but the person who does the will of my Father in heaven. When the day comes many will say to me, 'Lord, Lord, did we not prophesy in your name, cast out demons in your name, work many miracles in your name?'. Then I shall tell them to their faces: I have never known you; away from me, you evil men!" (Mt 7:21-23). Then Jesus uses the image of the foolish one who built his house on sand. The foundations failed when rain, floods and gales came. It was washed away. This is the one who does not build on obedience to God's word (Mt 7:24-26). We are to build on rock, so when the worst happens we will stand firm i.e., to listen to the words of Jesus and act on them. True discipleship, following his way, which is a narrow and tough path, brings assurance of salvation.

Hope for salvation of all

While insisting on the existence of hell, the Church has never declared any person to be actually in hell. The judgement must be left to God. Even though we might readily consider Hitler, Pol Pot, Stalin, Osama bin Laden, and other mass murderers as likely candidates, we must withhold judgement, which belongs to God alone. Of course, the general tradition of the Church has presumed Judas is in hell. After all Jesus did say of him "It would be better for that man if he had never been born" (Mt 26:24). Jesus also prayed to the Father that he had kept all those whom the Father had given him except the one who chose to be lost (Jn 17:12). At another time Jesus called Judas a devil (Jn 6:70).

It would be hard to make sense of these texts other than as an indication that Judas was in hell. Many saints believed this to be the case, including Augustine and Thomas Aquinas. However, even in this case we do better to withhold judgement. I don't see much point debating this issue. Pope Francis recently stirred the pot by suggesting the possibility that Judas may have ultimately been embraced by the mercy of God. But the Pope is aware there is no evidence for this. Even though the scriptural evidence does not favour Judas, we ought to leave the ultimate judgement to the Lord of all mercy.

Balthasar's challenge about the attitude of God and the blessed toward those in hell needs attention. The Fathers of the Church and saints have wrestled with this also. Gregory the Great maintained that "in heaven there will no longer be any compassion for misery" since there will be no misery. Peter Lombard takes this up and adds that the joy of heaven cannot be dampened. He argues their glories will be heightened as they see the punishments of the evil doers which they have escaped through the grace of God. But surely this explanation does not really satisfy us! How can those in heaven gloat over the previously loved ones on earth who are beyond salvation? Thomas Aquinas differs and softens the matter.[75] He argues that the blessed will definitely have compassion, since that is part of the experience of love, which is the experience of God. However, it is not a feeling of being impacted by the misery of the damned, such that they would want to change the situation. They trust fully in God's judgement.

While those in heaven have compassion and mercy for those on earth and seek to help them, once God's judgment has been made for eternity then the misery of those in hell is fixed and no further change is possible. Thomas denies that the saints in heaven would rejoice in the punishment of the wicked. However, they will be full of admiration for God's justice, and gratitude for their deliverance. Obviously this is a difficult issue. From my own humble and limited perspective it seems Thomas comes closest to explaining things. For me it is an obvious fact that God, together with the communion of saints in heaven, does actually continue to love those who are in hell. But the gulf that is between the blessed and damned is now impossible to cross, not because of God's will or that of the saints, but because of the will of those in hell who have chosen their lot. By their choice, as I have mentioned before, they would be more miserable in heaven than they are in hell. That is the great tragedy of their ultimate choice. Those in heaven are not gloating over the eternal loss of those in hell, but are, as with God himself, helpless to do anything about their plight. God is love, and all those caught up in God share his love. But as any parent knows the selfless love for your children can sometimes be rejected with tragic consequences. Using analogical language, we can say God's heart grieves over the lost. The victory of heaven is not a celebration of winners over losers, but an eternal praise of God for his saving love, which will not be dampened by those who have chosen to exclude themselves from this love.

Finally, I would claim that we certainly ought to hope that all will be saved. By this "hope" I do not mean a theological certainty, but a desire based on the reality of the victory of Christ's death and resurrection. We live with this hope; we live for this purpose. We labour tirelessly to bring the saving love of God to as many as possible. We know that only hearing the good news of Jesus, repenting, being baptised and committing one's life to him will anyone be assured of salvation. Yet we trust so many people, who through no fault of their own have not known Jesus, will be saved by the mercy of God. I have never met a person who is consummately evil; there is always a hidden thread of precious gold even in the most notorious criminal. We cannot judge; we must not judge. We must avoid estimates about how many are taking "the broad and spacious path to damnation". Our task is to reduce that number. But we must remain vigilant and unafraid to warn people who could easily be on a slippery slope. By hoping all will be saved I do not mean to presume this will inevitably be the outcome. All depends on the impenetrable mystery of God's grace and human freedom. While it is God's will for all to be saved, God has humbly made himself helpless in the face of wilful human obstinacy. The wonderful work of his saving love for every human person must be freely received. Human freedom is a wonderful and awesome gift. We must work strenuously to convince people to make the good choices, to opt for eternal life, not eternal death.

7

RESURRECTION OF THE BODY

Just as Christ is risen from the dead and lives forever, we live in the firm hope that after death those who have been faithful will live forever with the risen Christ and he will raise up our bodies on the last day. After death all will face immediate judgment. The souls of the faithful will go to God, possibly through the purification of purgatory. The souls of those who die in opposition to God will go to everlasting hell. On the last day God will resurrect the bodies of all. Those in heaven will be reunited with their bodies and find even greater blessing. Those in hell will also be reunited with their bodies but this will be an even greater source of affliction for them.

Faith in the resurrection

Belief in the resurrection of the dead has been central to Christian faith from the beginning. Paul insists: "How can some say that there is no resurrection of the dead? But if there is no resurrection for the dead, then Christ has not been raised; if Christ has not been raised, then our preaching is in vain and your faith is in vain" (1 Cor 15:12-13).

This faith in the resurrection of the dead developed gradually through the Old Testament. It reached explicit proclamation with the Maccabean martyrs, who were emboldened by the prospect of a joyful resurrection after being martyred rather than break the Law: "The King of the universe will raise us up to an everlasting renewal of life, because we have died for his laws" (2 Macc 7:9). At the time of Jesus the Pharisees firmly believed in the resurrection of the dead, but the Sadducees did not. Jesus rebuked the Sadducees for their blindness. He accused them of "not knowing the scriptures nor the power of God". Jesus corrects their image of God. He "is not God of the dead, but of the living" (Mk 12:24-27).

The surety of our resurrection from the dead is founded in the resurrection of Jesus himself. Jesus hung on the Cross in solidarity with the whole of sinful humanity. He died the death of all. As we have seen earlier, he made it possible for all who believe in him to die in a redeemed way. So, when Jesus rose from the dead he decisively defeated death's power over humanity. Just as all believers die in Christ, so all will share in the resurrection of his body. As Paul says, "For as in Adam all die, so also in Christ all will be made alive" (1 Cor 15:22). The meaning of death for humanity has been changed forever. The corruption of death has lost its power over humanity. The grave could not hold Christ. Nor can it hold all those united to him. All who die in Christ will rise in him. Upon death we trust our soul will go to God. Then on the last day, when the victory of Christ is complete, we will be bodily raised and live forever in our new glorified state. As Paul says, "For if we have been united with him in a death like his, we shall certainly be united with him in a resurrection like his" (Rom 6:5).

On the last day, through the power of Jesus' resurrection, God "will definitively grant incorruptible life to our bodies by reuniting them with our souls".[76] The body which has corrupted in the grave, or by other means, will be raised in a new glorified state. All of this will happen through the power of the resurrection of Jesus, and in the manner of the resurrection of Jesus. When Jesus was raised from the dead, he was not just a resuscitated corpse like Lazarus. Lazarus died again. The body of Jesus was glorified, shot through with the Holy Spirit. He would never die again. Death had been conquered. When the apostles met him, they knew something was radically different. He walked through walls and appeared anywhere at will. But he was not a phantom figure. He ate and drank with them. It was his real body, but glorified. So, in Christ, all will rise with their own bodies, but he will "change our lowly bodies to be like his glorious body".[77] Paul's describes this change as a seed which dies and brings new life. He explains:

> But someone will ask, 'How are the dead raised? With what kind of body do they come?' You foolish man! What you sow does not come to life unless it dies. And what you sow is not the body which is to be, but a bare kernel...What is dead will be raised imperishable... For this perishable nature must put on the imperishable, and this mortal nature must put on immortality (1 Cor 15:35-53).

What will our resurrected bodies be like?

We can't help being a little curious about what our glorified bodies will be like. The church's official teaching gives us no more than what I have already stated. That hasn't stopped saints and thinkers through the ages speculating. Thomas Aquinas has a whole section on this topic.[78] According to Aquinas our glorified bodies will still be identifiable as man and woman, but our sexuality will be glorified in such a way that marriage will be surpassed. Each person will have the same identity as on earth, but they will be transfigured into glory. The apostles never forgot the experience of the transfiguration of Jesus when his true identity became splendidly on display. They realised this was who Jesus really is. They were given an anticipation of his glorious resurrection, and a sign of what is in store for us in heaven. Each one in heaven will definitely be who he or she was in earthly existence, but changed, glorified. We will be able to recognise those we have known in the past, and they will recognise us.

Thomas also maintains that our bodies will be at their most perfect stage in nature. That would mean as in your prime! That is consoling. He calls this "integrity". One of the sorrows of this life is the reality of aging and the loss of physical powers. But in heaven we will be at the height of our powers. The good news is that our bodies will be whole. If you lost a leg through injury before dying, you will be fully intact. The bodies of those blessed in heaven will also be free from sickness, pain, or aging. He calls this impassibility. Nor will they be subject to bodily passions such as lust or hunger. We will have been perfected in holiness.

Thomas also suggests the bodies of the blessed will be perfectly coordinated, more than any athlete we have known. But the saints will not use their bodies on whim, but always in union with God's will. He says they will have the power to communicate their thoughts and feelings, the essence of who they are with ease and perfection. They will be totally holy, sharing fully in the fire of God's love, and sharing this love with one another. Because of this holiness they will be radiantly beautiful. He calls this clarity or luminosity. Light has always been associated with holiness. God is light and in him there is no darkness. So also for those who live fully in the light of God. They share fully in his holiness, shining splendidly. Our bodies will not in any way hinder expressing who we are to others. Rather we will be totally transparent in giving of self to the other. In heaven there will be no secrets. Rather everyone will know all about one another with a glance. Our bodies will be illuminated by the light of God and will express perfectly who we are. This will be the basis of the perfect communion of the blessed in God.

Resurrection now

There is a danger in this speculation about what our bodies will be like in heaven, focussing on what joys will be ours. It may suggest that all we need to do is just wait for that great day when Jesus will come in a cloud of glory to snatch us up with him to live forever in joyful bliss. That would be a rather self-centred perspective, not true to scriptural revelation. Heaven after all is not all about us, but it is all about God, and us being caught up in the love of God for all. Our desire for heaven should not distract us from the urgent call to focus on changing the world now. On the other hand, it would be short-sighted to be so preoccupied with the earthly slog, not to keep an eye on eternity. The Church down through the centuries has been rightly fascinated with our supernatural goal and the perfection yet to come. Gaining great hope in anticipation of what is yet to come can motivate us to evangelise and build a better world here.

The scriptural teaching on our resurrection is not only about regaining our glorified bodies at the end of time. In Paul's perspective we *already* experience resurrection of our bodies in baptism. By the "body" Paul does not just mean the material component of our being which is animated by the soul. He means the human person in its entirety, one's identity. We are body-persons, or some-body. The body is the person as he or she is in history, responsible for what he or she does, for how he or she lives. It is one's personality.[79] This body of ours in this sense needs to undergo transformation now, not just at the end.

In baptism we are buried with Christ and Paul assures us "by baptism too you have been raised up with him through your belief in the power of God who raised him from the dead" (Col 2:12). Paul tells us God "raised us up with him and gave us a place with him in heaven, in Christ Jesus" (Eph 2:5-6). We are in a process of appropriating the resurrection of Christ into our lives. As we die to ourselves and live for others, we "put on Christ". The new resurrection life in Christ is growing in us. It has not yet reached its fullness. Paul is very intent upon the power of Christ's resurrection for us now. In baptism we were joined with him in the tomb as it were, and then we rose with him. We already experience "bodily" resurrection. The whole Christian life of holiness entails embracing more deeply the power of Christ's resurrection and living already the victory he has won for us (Rom 6:1-11). Arguably, this perspective on bodily resurrection is more central to Paul's thinking than what happens at the end of time.[80]

Resurrection experience

A married man addicted to on-line pornography hears a preaching which convinces him of the need to change and by

God's grace he *can* change. The porn has been slowly sapping the joy out of his relationship with his wife. He lives in terror of her discovering his enslavement. Now he realises the possibility of freedom. He seeks prayer ministry, opening up his shame, allowing the Spirit to reveal a hidden trauma of the past, and the lies he has been fed by the evil one. He makes a decisive break with the sinful pattern, and puts in place various practical measures to protect him from recidivist behaviour. Victory in Christ, from death to resurrection! Paul says, "For all who are in Christ Jesus there is a new creation. The old is gone and the new is here" (2Cor 5:17). We do not have to allow the devil to deceive us and confuse us about our true identity. The "father of lies" whispers into the heart deceptive ideas that can keep us captive "you are doomed to repeat your failures again and again; there is no future for you". But, in contrast, the Father of life through the Spirit at work in the heart speaks to us of a "future full of hope".

A middle-aged woman is full of bitterness and resentment. After an inheritance battle over the parents' estate, she was left with very little compared to her siblings. Devastated, she was intent on revenge. Full of anger and hate she was preparing for a mammoth court battle, which would be prolonged for years. Realising the deadly grip of vengeance in her heart she seeks advice from a priest. He listens compassionately, but gently reminds her of the way Jesus warned us not to allow avarice to grip our hearts, and especially not to allow unforgiveness to be like a deadly cancer in the soul. After much sharing and prayer, she owns the reality of her captivity. Drawing upon the grace of her baptism, she forgives, and is set free. Even though she knew she could possibly win the court case due to the injustice done, she decides to let it go for her own sake and that of others. Life is too short to spend in enmity and vicious quarrelling. Another experience from death to life. Under the influence of the Spirit she is already anticipating the ultimate resurrection on the last day.

Eternal life

John's teaching on eternal life in his gospel has a similar message. Eternal life for John is not primarily a state in the future which we wait to receive after death. Those who listen to the words of Jesus and believe in the one who sent Jesus have eternal life already (Jn 5:24). The Father's will is to raise up anyone who believes in the Son, and that person already possesses eternal life (Jn 6:40,47). Jesus declared to Martha: "I am the resurrection and the life. If anyone believes in me, even though he dies he will live, and whoever lives and believes in me will never die. Do you believe this?" (Jn 11:25-26). A question Jesus asks of each one of us. When we answer affirmatively, the end of time is already upon us. Heaven is already breaking into our life here and now.

A young man comes for counselling. He hates his dad who is a chronic alcoholic and has spent time in jail. He is now working for his dad in the family business, but almost daily there are bursts of anger and embittered arguments between them. He has childhood memories of his father's alcohol-fuelled violence towards his mum. Once during his teens his dad in a rage threatened to kill him. He believes in Jesus, and is desperate for the Lord's help. The priest helps him to identify all the traumatic moments of the past, especially in relation to his dad. Then he leads the young man to ask forgiveness of the Lord for his own rage and for the times he wished his dad was dead. From there he helps the young man decide to forgive his father, recognising that it is a process, but he needs to start exercising his free will to forgive. With copious tears, the young man does so. Then the priest helps the young man identify all the lies of the enemy which he has imbibed, such as "I will never be happy in life", "the only way I can get respect from people is to rage", "my worth depends on getting the better of people", and other negative tapes that run through his brain. He is encouraged to renounce each of these lies. The priest takes authority over all evil spirits that may be afflicting the lad. Then he prays for the Holy Spirit to fill this young guy with an abundance of love and new life. Transformation! Resurrection! Eternal life already present in the soul! Joy, peace, light and love!

So our human resurrection is not only the reanimation of our bodies from the grave at the end of time, but a process that begins with baptism, is extended through our earthly pilgrimage as we grow more in Christ, experienced immediately after death by those who have lived and died in Christ and will reach a fullness when the Lord comes again and we will be in our glorious bodies with the whole cosmos being renewed.

The promise of Eucharist

Jesus said, "Anyone who eats my flesh and drinks my blood has eternal life, and I shall raise him up on the last day" (Jn 6:54). We have such an enormous privilege in regularly participating in Eucharist, which already is an anticipation of the glory that is to come. Every time we celebrate Eucharist we are told by Ignatius of Antioch we "break the one bread that provides the medicine of immortality, the antidote for death, and the food that makes us live for ever in Jesus Christ".[81] In the Eucharist we are joining the whole church which is constantly calling for the coming of the Lord: "Maranatha! Come, Lord Jesus!" (Rev 22:20).

By our sharing in the Eucharist we are being fashioned into what we eat. When we consume other food, it is assimilated into the body, and some ends up in the sewer. In Eucharist the opposite happens. When we consume the body of the Lord, we are assimilated into him. As Pope Benedict explained, "my 'I' is assimilated to that of Jesus, it is made similar to him in an exchange that increasingly breaks through the lines of division".[82] Instead of this sacred food of the body of the Lord being assimilated into our bodies, he assimilates us into his body. Thus, the Eucharist becomes the means of our resurrection. The Eucharist feeds us with God's life, healing us, transforming us into the likeness of Christ. Through this communion our mortal bodies are imbued with the capacity to be divinised and glorified through the resurrected body of Christ. That is why the Eucharist is recommended by the Church as the last sacrament for the dying, as holy Viaticum, providing the "passing over" to the Father. As the Catechism says, the Eucharist is "the seed of eternal life and the power of the resurrection."[83]

This may explain why most of the appearances of the Risen Jesus in the gospels are in the context of a meal. The appearances on the beach in Galilee, the Upper room, on the road to Emmaus, all have a Eucharistic theme. Jesus breaks the bread and feeds his apostles. It is a sign to them that his body, now risen, is available to them in a new way. His body has been changed into glory. When we partake of him, the living bread of heaven, we gain the capacity to be glorified, and to be resurrected on the last day. He is the "living bread come down from heaven". Anyone who eats of this bread will live forever. The promise will be fulfilled. The one who eats the flesh of the Son of man and drinks his blood will be raised up on the last day (Jn 6:51-54).

8
THE SECOND COMING

Hope

As the previous chapter proclaimed, Christian hope is not only based on what is to come in the future. Our hope is grounded first and foremost on what we already experience in Christ. We have been baptised into his death and resurrection, sharing in the victory he has won over sin and death. We can rejoice in eternal life which is already present within us. We share in the Eucharist which deepens us in union with the risen Christ. We are active members of the body of Christ, drawing grace upon grace from this ambience of love. We are sons and daughters of the living Father through the Spirit who dwells within us. Peter assures us we have a "sure hope and promise of an inheritance that can never be spoilt or soiled or fade away, because it is being kept for us in the heavens" (1 Pet 1:4). Peter is writing to the newly baptised and he reinforces this message within them, "Through your faith, God's power will guard you until the salvation which has been prepared is revealed at the end of time" (1 Pet 1:5). Because of their firsthand experience of the risen Christ through baptism, even though they will endure many hardships, like gold being refined in the fire, they will be filled with indescribable joy. Even though they did not see with their own eyes the risen body of Christ, they know and love him, who is the salvation of their lives.

Through our encounter with the risen Christ we have already experienced resurrection within us, and this is our hope. We are not talking about some sort of wishful thinking or a vague dream that all will be well. Christ is risen. He is Lord of our lives. Sin cannot dominate us anymore. He has broken the power of sin and death. Our eternity begins now. The Holy Spirit dwells within us and acts as a down-payment (*arrabon* in Greek), a first instalment, a pledge, a seal that we carry in our hearts (2 Cor 1:22). As Paul assures the Ephesians, "you too have been stamped with the seal of the Holy Spirit of the Promise, the pledge (*arrabon*) of our inheritance, which brings freedom for those whom God has taken for his own, to make his glory praised" (Eph 1:14). We have been claimed by the love of God. This is our identity; chosen, consecrated and set apart for his wonderful work within this world.

The parousia

Our experience of the kingdom is already wonderful, but not yet fully accomplished in us. When a person purchases a car, they often give the dealer a down-payment and say, "I will be back". In a similar way the Lord gives his down-payment and promises, "I will return!" The guarantee has been given, and paid for with his own blood, and sealed in his resurrection. But he will come back to complete what has been done already. When Christ first came as the incarnate Son of God, he was as the humble lamb of God who was taken to the slaughter-house for our sake, the suffering one for our salvation. But when he returns, he will come in majesty and glory as the Lord of all. Jesus paints the startling picture of his return: "The sign of the Son of man will appear in heaven; then too all the peoples of the earth will beat their breasts; and they will see the Son of Man coming on the clouds of heaven with great power and great glory" (Mt 24:30).

No one will miss his return in majesty, which we call the parousia, "because the coming of the Son of Man will be like lightning striking in the east and flashing far into the west" (Mt 24:27). He will come at a time when people least expect (Mt 24:37-41). So it is incumbent on all to stay awake, be ready, and have our lives in good order. Jesus told the parable about the irresponsible stewards who were not faithful in their service and were caught unready (Mt 24:45-51). He also told the parable of the five wise bridesmaids who brought enough oil with them to keep their lamps burning in case the bridegroom was late in coming, while the five foolish did not. We must wait responsibly by keeping the oil of Holy Spirit, the fire of God's love, burning in our hearts at all times and seasons. Other parables also make the same point.

These parables are not accidental to Jesus' teaching but right at the centre of the gospel. We must live as if the parousia is imminent, ready at any moment for the Lord's coming. But we are not to speculate or try to predict when it will happen. Jesus told his apostles, "It is not for you to know times or seasons which the Father has fixed by his own authority" (Acts 1:7). The doomsday prophets who believe they can predict when the Lord will come are suffering from self-deception. Jesus says it will come suddenly, like a trap which snares its game, or like a burglar who comes unexpectedly in the night. "Therefore, you too must stand ready because the Son of Man is coming at an hour you do not expect" (Mt 24:44).

Signs of the second coming

The *Catholic Catechism* teaches us that there will be some significant events preceding the second coming. Firstly, there will be considerable softening of heart by the Jewish people to the recognition of Jesus as the Messiah. Paul taught their acceptance of Christ would usher in the resurrection from the dead (Rom 11:15). Secondly, the Church will go through a final trial under persecution which will shake the faith of many believers. Jesus warns "You will be betrayed even by parents and brothers, relations and friends; and some of you will be put to death. You will be hated by all people on account of my name, but not a hair of your head will be lost. Your endurance will win you your lives" (Lk 21:14-15). Thirdly, as part of this final trial the anti-Christ will appear and deceive humanity: "a pseudo-messianism by which man glorifies himself in place of God and of his Messiah come in the flesh".[84] The Church will go through this final trial as a deepening in the death and resurrection of Jesus. The kingdom will not be fulfilled by the Church's ascendancy, but by the victory of Christ himself over the final unleashing of evil. This will be accompanied by the judgement of the living and dead.

We should note that in the gospel texts on the second coming Jesus uses apocalyptic language. The Greek word *apokalupsis* means taking away the veil. Jesus speaks of cosmic upheaval, where the sun will be darkened, the moon will show no light, stars will fall from the sky, and all the heavenly hosts shaken (Mt 24:29-30). We don't have to imagine it happening as a tumultuous, universal cataclysm. The language is symbolic. The sun, moon and stars for the ancients were the means by which ships navigated. Even traveling on land these heavenly bodies were primary indicators of direction. For them to be falling out of the sky, means metaphorically our social, moral, and political universe is shaken. All our current presumptions by which we establish our bearings in life, are overturned.

Jesus is proclaiming that the day is coming when the way we typically navigate through life will be upended. All of the certainties that we currently rely upon will be in turmoil – the accepted cultural systems, the world of ideas, the forces by which we live our lives, all will be in turmoil, and we will be able to rely on nothing but God. The shake-up of all systems of power in the light of the coming of the Lord will bring us all to our knees. We will be violently shaken out of our complacency. All political and social systems will be reduced to subservience. The whole world system will be turned upside down. It will be more disturbing than any catastrophe of the physical order. The whole of humanity will come to realise our subjection to God Almighty.

Misguided "apocalyptic" mentality

In historical times of uncertainty and disruption pious, conscientious people can be prone to an unfortunate "apocalyptic" fear. The current widespread loss of faith in God within Western countries, and the consequent development of a culture which has lost its moral bearings, witnessed by acceptance of abortion, euthanasia, gay marriage and the like, has left many feeling insecure and uncertain about the future. In this context a hard-core Catholic fundamentalism has sprouted. Fear is fed by websites encouraging adherents to prepare for the last battle.[85] In this time of crisis two responses manifest.[86] Firstly, there are those who will aggressively fight the "culture wars" with a vengeance, warning all to prepare for the imminent justice of an Armageddon, a final showdown between the forces of good and evil. In this mentality there is no point in working for peace and justice to bring change to the world. It is too late. The time has come. The crisis is upon us. The absolute imperative now is to be ready for the final battle against the Enemy. Secondly, there are those who are not persuaded by the "call to arms" but withdraw into ghettos or pockets of loyal adherents to prepare spiritually for the coming of the Lord. They largely give up on the earthly enterprise as a lost cause and wait expectantly for the end. There is no point trying to change the world. It is all too late. There is only a short time left to gather in our sectarian circle, store up provisions, and wait upon the coming of the chastisement of the Lord.

Various private revelations are marshalled to bolster this "call to arms" or retreat into the desert. The end time prophets warn of an imminent chastisement, followed by a rise of the Antichrist, and then the arrival of universal "era of peace", during which Satan will be chained for a thousand years. All of this they claim is described by Revelations 20:1-3. Their misinterpretation of the Book of Revelations, which was originally called The Book of the Apocalypse, and failure to understand the purpose of the book compounds the issue. While Catholic proponents of this mentality deny millenarianism they unfortunately can fall into a contemporary version of this perversion of truth. They believe that after the struggle against evil has reached its climax, and the anti-Christ has been overcome, there will come an extended era of peace on earth when the Church will prevail triumphantly. Christ will reign by a spiritual supremacy in the hearts of all. The kingdom of God will have come to earth in completion and we will all be fulfilling the will of God. To hasten the arrival of this time God needs more of us to prepare with our hearts and be ready.

Two points need to be made in regard to these speculations about the Second Coming. Firstly, Jesus makes it patently clear that we must not anticipate the hour of his coming, since this is known only to the Father. When people do make prophecies we are to ignore them. "If, then, they say to you, 'Look, he is in the desert', do not go there; 'Look, he is in some hiding place', do not believe it; because the coming of the Son of Man will be like lightning striking in the east and flashing far into the west" (Mt 24:26-27). He urges us to "stay awake, because you do not know the day when your master is coming…" (Mt 24:42). He is adamant that his second coming will be totally unexpected. For that reason we must stand ready at all times. We are to live always on the edge of his arrival. No particular historical circumstances should dictate to us a special time of urgency. Every day is meant to be lived as if the Lord was coming tomorrow.

Secondly, the proponents of these doctrines skirt closely to millenarianism, which is the proposal that Christ will return in the flesh to establish a millennial kingdom on earth. They claim this is not the case. Yet the Catholic Catechism applies the term millenarianism to any attempt to create a form of earthly paradise before the Second Coming. The Catechism condemns "secular messianism", the idea that a secular state can fulfill the role of the messiah though the creation of an earthly utopia. The Catechism says,

> The Antichrist's deception already begins to take shape in the world every time the claim is made to realise within history that messianic hope which can only be realized beyond history through the eschatological judgment. The Church has rejected even modified forms of this falsification of the kingdom to come under the name of millenarianism.[87]

While some of the modern Christian speculations look to political figures to be the fulfillment of their messianic hopes, it is fair to say that most don't go that far. The Catechism is directly condemning the sort of millenarianism which gave birth of the communist and fascist movements of the 20th century. Nevertheless, many contemporary end-time adherents are expecting a time of earthly paradise before the coming of the Lord. How could this come about without a total conversion of the world? How could it happen before God's judgement is made? Anyway, regardless of whether they are millenarian or not, all of these end-time speculations do not really serve the gospel but mislead good people into pathways of endless anxiety and useless seclusion from the world, which avoids the commission of Jesus to go make disciples of all nations. Rather than down tools and enter the ark to await the coming flood, they would do better to be filled with the Holy Spirit and bring this fire to the earth through evangelisation and works of mercy.

Misinterpretation of the Book of Revelations

Common to all current "end time" prophecies is an erroneous interpretation of the Book of Revelations. In common language today the Greek term apocalypse has come to denote the coming of the Lord at the end of time. But, as was mentioned earlier, it simply means an "unveiling". The book was written to a people under persecution, unveiling the awesome significance of the death and resurrection of Jesus Christ.[88] The author's intention was not primarily to give us hidden insight into the circumstances surrounding the last day and the Parousia. The author was more intent upon the present state of Christians as they experienced persecution under the violence and destructive forces of the Roman Empire. His purpose was not to give us hidden knowledge about the times and manner of the coming of the Lord, but to encourage Christians who were facing martyrdom to hold steadfast and know that the ultimate victory is with the Lamb who was slain for us and now reigns in heavenly glory. The book is not primarily about the physical cosmos coming to an end, nor about the end of world history. While the author gives a riveting picture of what will precede the second coming of the Lord and wants his readers to be expectant and ready for the tumult of the last times, he is not sounding a fearful alarm. Rather, he is making a resounding proclamation that the good news of Jesus Christ will prevail over every destructive force brought against it.

The author, probably John the apostle, on the island of Patmos was writing to the churches under persecution emboldening them with the truth. He proclaims that the old world of Roman domination and subjugation of the Church will pass away. A new world is emerging which will be centred in the acknowledgement that Jesus is Lord. The whole book is an image-laden meditation on the awesome power of the Resurrection of Jesus Christ, which has altered human history forever. He is encouraging his readers not to be afraid, but to take courage because Jesus, the risen Lord is the Alpha and Omega, the beginning and the end of all history. The power of the Roman Empire which put Jesus to death has been overcome. The old world is receding and the new one is coming. The Church's task in any age is to let the world know that victory has come in Jesus Christ. They will be kept safe in the time of trial. Martyrdom is a victory. The beleaguered early communities of Christians under persecution could rejoice. In the light of the resurrection of Jesus there is a greater more powerful army of every race and tribe and language (Rev 7:1-8). This is represented by the vision of heaven populated by the 144,000 marked with the seal of the New Israel, the Church, representing all the martyrs down through the line of history, in contrast with the limited Roman army tattooed with the sign of the emperor, which will soon fade from history. A great heavenly array of people clothed in white robes and palm branches in hands (code for martyrs) is worshipping the Lamb who was slain and has now gained victory (Rev 7:9-10).

John's vision is not for people to desire to escape this earth as soon as they can, but to cooperate with the creation of a new world which is coming about through the resurrection of Christ. The definitive victory over the powers of evil and darkness has been won. The chaotic powers that have worked against humanity due to sin have now been overcome. The whole of the created world can be made new. We can cooperate with the creation of this new world by whole-heartedly worshipping God, loving our neighbours, caring for the poor. God has done the work. We join him in bringing the new heaven and the new earth: "Then I saw a new heaven and a new earth, the first heaven and the first earth had disappeared now, and there was no longer any sea. I saw the holy city, and the new Jerusalem, coming down from God out of heaven, as beautiful as a bride all dressed for her husband. Then I heard a loud voice call from the throne, 'You see this city? Here God lives with us'" (Rev 21:1-8). The sea, representing chaos in the ancient mind, has gone. All is made new. This is not a proclamation of the need to escape from earth as soon as possible. Rather, it announces God coming to us, the marriage of heaven and earth. The church is prepared as a bride adorned for her husband, who has come to marry himself to us.

The Book of the Apocalypse has been misused by many seeking to fit its imagery into their own fearful proclamation of the imminent coming of the Lord. They miss the point of the book. The author proclaims that the chaos of the sinful world, represented by the immediate destructive forces of Roman imperialism, has been overcome. Victory belongs to all who have given their lives to Christ. Already the Church's worship, especially in the celebration of Eucharist, unveils the worship of the Risen Christ in heaven. John gives us the startling image of the countless saints "from every nation, race, tribe and language" before the throne in front of the Lamb, dressed in white robes and holding palms in their hands shouting, "Victory to our God, who sits on the throne, and to the Lamb!" And all around the throne were bowing in adoration, worshipping God with these words, "Amen. Praise and glory and wisdom and thanksgiving and honour and power and strength to our God for ever and ever" (Rev 7:12). Those who worship "the beast" will be damned, but those who worship the living God, who join in the Church's right praise and adoration of the Lamb who was crucified and now is risen, will prevail. This was true for the first Christians. It is true for the Church in every age until the Lord comes again.

Significance of the last judgement

Returning to consideration of the Parousia, we need to reflect more on the significance of the universal judgement of the living and the dead. All will be raised bodily and brought before the judgement seat of God. When we think about the last judgement it is important to remember that the particular judgement has already occurred. We will already have been judged worthy of heaven or hell. There will be no appeal court. So, what does the last judgement bring? It is a moment of truth like none other. It could potentially be a "cringe" moment for many of us, since everything about our lives and our relationship with God will be laid bare. But, if we have already been through the cleansing grace of purgatory, our dark wounds will already be healed. The truth will set us free. Being confronted with reality will not undo us. The glorious Christ will reveal the secret disposition of our hearts and we will see how perfect his judgement is, rendering each one their due according to our works and according to our acceptance or refusal of grace.

The Catechism says the last judgement "will reveal even to its furthest consequences the good each has done or failed to do during this earthly life".[89] The truth of each person's relationship with God will be laid bare. Everything we have said, thought or done will be for all to see. There will be no room for a stance of pride, and we will see more clearly that any advance in grace has only been because of the mercy of God. But neither will there be any room for shame since we will be full of gratitude for God's immense mercy which has saved us. We will be able to see how the hidden hand of God has been in our lives even when we did not recognise it. As the Catechism says we will see the "furthest consequences of our actions". We will see how a word we spoke may have touched the heart of another and brought them to salvation, how tragedies that happened were used by God to bring good which we never realised, how every choice we made may have affected others either for good or for bad.

We will not only be confronted with the truth of our own journey with God, but we will also know the full story of every other human being. We will know them as we are known. And they will know all about us as well. We will see how we have misjudged people, how we have failed to appreciate the goodness of those we have spurned, how we may have been blinded by our own prejudices and not realised the favour of God on them. We will see how some who we thought to be quintessentially holy were far from saintly, and maybe even a fraud. Nothing will be left hidden. All will be laid bare. We will see the exquisite mercy of God in his relationship with people, and we will see how just he is in judging every person.

The reality of judgement

We discussed the issue of judgement earlier in chapter two. We know that Jesus often spoke of judgement as a warning for us to prepare well for his coming. Some of these warnings can be confronting. For example, "The Son of Man will send his angels and they will gather out of his kingdom all causes of sin and all evil-doers, and throw them into the furnace of fire; there will be weeping and grinding of teeth" (Mt 13:41-42). What can we make of this? Surely we cannot explain it away, nor trivialise it. There is a real warning here. But we need to shed light on texts like this so we understand them correctly.

Firstly we need to realise that God always acts according to who God is. Now "God is love" (1 Jn 4:8). God is "the Lord, a God merciful and gracious, persistent in passionate concern, abounding in steadfast love and faithfulness" (Ex 34:6). God is just because he always acts according to his faithful love. Everything God does is an expression of his love, which is unconditional and perfect. Paul says, "what proves that God loves us is that Christ died for us while we were still sinners" (Rom 5:12). The problem is that we often act against God's will. We use our own free will to sin. If we are acting unjustly, God knows. We cannot deceive God.

God does not force his love on us. If he did, it would not be love. In the story of the prodigal son the father was rich in mercy, but the son had to come to his senses. Until he decided to return, he remained in the pig sty. We can create our own pig sty and refuse to exercise our freedom to get out of it. If we reject God's love, turn our backs upon his wisdom and his will, we must suffer the consequences. The Scriptures talk about God punishing the sinner, but in reality we punish ourselves when we refuse to repent. "Your wickedness will chasten you, and your apostasy will reprove you. Know and see that it is evil and bitter for you to forsake the Lord your God" (Jer 2:19). God does not directly inflict punishment (even though the bible uses this language). It is our sin which causes the evil and traps us. Sin is contrary to what God desires for each of us, and a rejection of the grace given by God's love. Our sin separates us from God and we experience it as punishment. But it is self-inflicted.

When Scripture talks about "the wrath of God" or "the anger of God" we must be careful not to think this refers to a hatred or distaste as an emotional reaction in the heart of God. The analogical language can convey the wrong concept of God. It simply declares the objective reality that the holiness of God cannot abide with sin. Jesus, took upon himself the punishment due to our sins when he hung on the Cross for our sake, so that we could walk free. His love is totally given for us. There is no holding back, no withdrawing. But as an expression of his love, he has given us freedom, which means we are not puppets on his string. We have inestimable dignity due to this gift of freedom. But by its very nature we can abuse this gift. In extreme cases that could mean eternal separation from God. As mentioned in chapter 6, God sends no one to hell. If anyone goes to hell it will be because of their own intransigence and due to the disfigurement of their sin. They will not want to be in heaven, they could not stand being in the presence of God. Eternal separation from God due to refusal to accept his love is what we call hell. God grieves the eternal loss of any person who he has created, and for whom he died on the Cross, but because of who he is, he cannot force someone to choose heaven. Hell has a door locked from the inside. The great tragedy is that some would rather reign in hell than serve in heaven.

9

A NEW HEAVEN AND A NEW EARTH

We do not know the time for the end of human history and the consummation of the world. Yet our faith assures us that Christ will eventually return in glory, and after judging the living and the dead, God the Father will bring about a "new heaven and a new earth". Not only will we be transformed at the end of time by bodily resurrection; the Church as the body of Christ will be transformed into glory, and "the universe itself will be renewed".[90]

At the end of time the Church will finally be cleansed of all its impurities and become the bride perfected in glory. As Vatican II proclaimed:

> The Church, to which we are all called in Christ Jesus, and in which by the grace of God we attain holiness, will receive its perfection only in the glory of heaven, when together with the human race, the universe itself, which is closely related to humanity, and which through it attains its destiny, will be perfectly established in Christ.[91]

The Church, sacrament of salvation

This restoration has already begun in Christ to the extent that the Church is the "universal sacrament of salvation", constantly seeking to draw people into Christ through the work of the Holy Spirit. We already live in the final age (1 Cor 10:11). The Church, to the extent that it is being faithful to its calling, is already an anticipation of what is to come. However, the pilgrim church still "carries the mark of this world which will pass" and with all of humanity groans in travail for the fullness yet to come.

Within the plan of God, the Church is the sacrament of the unity of the whole human race.[92] Unfortunately, we are often an obscure sign of what we could and should be. But the reality remains that the Church in all its weakness and sinfulness carries the seed and some of the growth of the kingdom which will come to full flowering at the end of time. The consummation to come will be "the final realisation of the unity of the human race, which God willed from creation".[93]

Those who have been welcomed into heaven, united fully with Christ, will form the communion of the redeemed. The vision of John in Revelations, describing the new heaven and new earth, speaks of the "holy city, and the new Jerusalem, coming down from God out of heaven, as beautiful as a bride all dressed for her husband" (Rev 21:2). The Church will no longer be wounded by sin, arrogance, self-seeking ambition, pride, lust, or evil of any kind. Given our present experience of Church in the throes of scandals of all kinds, this vision seems almost far-fetched, too hard to imagine. But this is our sure hope, grounded in God's promise. The Church will be renewed in pristine purity, freed from its corruption and rendered spotless, "the Bride the Lamb has married" (Rev 21:9).

Renewal of the Cosmos

In a splendid way, far beyond our wildest imaginings, the whole of the cosmos will be renewed. Not only will human beings be brought to perfection, but also the whole of creation will be made new in Christ. In a wonderful passage in Romans Paul proclaims:

> I think that what we suffer now cannot be compared to the glory yet to be revealed, which awaits us. The whole of creation is eagerly waiting for God to reveal his sons and daughters. It was not for any fault on the part of creation that it was made unable to attain its purpose, it was made so by God; but creation still retains the hope of being freed, like us, from its slavery to decadence, to enjoy the same freedom and glory as the children of God. From the beginning until now the entire creation, as we know, has been groaning in one great act of giving birth; and not only creation, but all of us who possess the first-fruits of the Spirit, we too groan inwardly as we await for our bodies to be set free (Rom 8:18-23).

Paul is helping us get in touch with the deep longing in each of us for universal communion in God. We, together with the whole of creation, groan deeply within us as we yearn for the fullness for which we are made. Later Paul will speak about prayer as not so much sprouting many words, but a deep yearning for God, which is the work of the Spirit within us. He says the Spirit comes to our aid in our weakness when words cannot possibly express what is within us. The Spirit will express our pleas in "groans too deep for words", and these pleas are always according to the mind of God (Rom 8:28-29). We are in union with the whole of creation, which has also lost its perfect harmony because of sin. We yearn for the deepest freedom of the sons and daughters of God, which has been won by Jesus' redeeming work, but not yet brought to completion.

Universal restoration

God's purpose is to restore the visible universe. The whole world groans for this ultimate redemption. We do not know the way the universe will be transformed. But it will not be annihilated. St Irenaeus, championing the truth of the resurrection of the body and its connection to the renewal of creation insists on its transformation, "so that the world itself, restored to its original state, facing no further obstacles, should be at the service of the righteous".[94] He continues

> Neither the substance nor the essence of the creation will be annihilated, for the one who established it is faithful and true, but 'the present form of this world is passing away' (1 Cor 7:31) – that is, all that in which transgression has occurred … But when this present fashion of things passes away, and humanity has been renewed and flourishes in an incorruptible state … then the new heaven and the new earth will exist, in which a new humanity will remain forever, always communing with God.[95]

This vision is faithful to the true meaning of the resurrection of the body and puts paid to doomsday predictions of the end being one big explosion disintegrating everything. God's creation is precious to him. He is preparing "a new dwelling and a new earth in which righteousness dwells".[96] He will build "an everlasting home in the heavens, not made by human hands" (2 Cor 5:1).

All of creation will be set free from its bondage to decay. There will be a new heaven and a new earth. Isaiah saw this in prophetic vision when he envisaged a new order in the universe, when the Holy Spirit will make all things new, a fresh time of justice for the oppressed, peace in the whole of creation, a unity amongst all people, when all our deepest longings will be fulfilled (Is 11: 1-9). John saw this new heaven and new earth in his vision of the new Jerusalem in which the "river of life" will flow from the throne of God and the Lamb. Drawing from imagery of the river flowing out of Eden to water the garden in original paradise (Gen 2:10), and the water gushing out from below the threshold of the temple in Ezekiel's vision of a medicinal, saving stream for all, John envisages a new paradise, a world transformed by the glory of God.

In Colossians Paul presents an ancient Christian hymn celebrating that all things in heaven and earth were created in Christ and for him. "Before anything was created he existed and he holds all things in unity." Then Paul speaks about the new creation brought about through Christ's redeeming work. "He was the first to be born from the dead" (Col 1:17-18). By the power of his resurrection, "God wanted all things to be reconciled through him and for him, everything in heaven and everything on earth when he made peace by his death on the cross" (Col 1:20). What an extraordinary universal vision! The shape this is to take defies our imagination. We are left to wonder, to yearn for the fullness yet to come, to let paltry dreams and petty squabbles fade into insignificance, and to wait expectantly for the new heaven and the new earth.

10
LET US PROCLAIM THE GOOD NEWS

An eternal perspective

An eternal perspective sharpens our proclamation of the Good News. We feel a new urgency. Every person needs to know the ultimate purpose of their lives, the end God desires for each one of us. Everyone needs to taste now what is yet to come to completion in the future. Every human being needs to know the saving love of God revealed in Jesus Christ. This is the ultimate way of being human now and the path towards fullness of life forever. As Paul says, "All I want is to know Christ and the power of his resurrection and to share his sufferings by reproducing the pattern of his death. That is why I can hope to take my place in the resurrection of the dead" (Phil 3:10-11). He goes on to say that he is far from perfect now, but he is still running the race "trying to capture the prize for which Christ Jesus captured me". He is far from presuming he has already won the race. But he is straining ahead for the future yet to come. He is focused on the ultimate goal: "I am racing for the finish, for the prize to which God calls us upwards to receive in Christ Jesus" (Phil 3:14).

No doubt the fact that Paul was in prison when writing this letter to the Philippians, made him acutely aware that his hold on this life is precarious. He had earlier shared vulnerably with his friends that he was wrestling within himself (Phil 1:21-26). Should he pray to be taken into glory now through martyrdom? Or should he pray to stay longer for the sake of the mission at hand? He finds the first option alluring because he would be with Christ forever. He had already proclaimed "For me to live is Christ; but to die is gain" (Phil 1:21) But the second outcome is more immediately compelling for Paul, since he loves his people and wants to see them grow in their faith and evangelizing fervour. For Paul the whole Christian life is simply to proclaim joyfully the good news of Christ in season and out of season; "to make the preaching of the good news one's life's work in thorough-going service" (2 Tim 4:5).

Stewards of Christ

Paul tells us we are simply stewards of this mystery of Christ. As stewards we are commissioned to bring this good news to all. Paul, himself, had received a compelling vision of the Risen Christ. Consequently, he was convinced he must proclaim God's love to all. "I have been made a servant of that gospel by a gift of grace from God who gave it to me by his own power" (Eph 3:7). He encourages us to be good stewards also as we await the second coming of the Lord. A steward is someone entrusted by the Master with a precious gift which must be protected and not squandered. The gift is the experiential knowledge of "the infinite treasure of Christ". The only way to be a good steward of this gift is to bring it to as many people as possible before we die. When the Lord comes again he will want us to be fully engaged in this sacred task entrusted to us.

What has been so generously given to us, namely the saving grace of God in Jesus Christ, was not only for ourselves. We are entrusted with this grace so, as good stewards, we will bring this good news to others. Paul begs us not to squander the grace given to us, not to waste the gift by neglecting to share it with others. We are "ambassadors for Christ; it is as though God were appealing through us, and the appeal that we make in Christ's name is: be reconciled to God" (2Cor 5:20). This is the favourable time; not later when we may feel more ready; no, now is the day of salvation. This is the anointed and appointed time to proclaim salvation won for us through the crucified and risen Lord.

Jesus likens our task to that of servants inviting people to the wedding feast of the king's son (Mt 22:1-14), or to a festive banquet prepared for many people (Lk 14:1-24). In each of these parables the most significant feature is the determination of the king to have the banquet hall full. The word must go out to all and sundry, "The wedding is ready! Come to the wedding!" The urgent call must go out far and wide. Come to the banquet! Even if people do not listen to the invitation, or procrastinate in response, or simply walk away, we are not to be discouraged. Rejection lends more urgency to the invitation. Now is the time for response. Come to the banquet before it is too late. Our contemporaries need to hear the invitation, not as a threat but as a fantastic opportunity to a more fulfilled life now and forever. Jesus has come to offer 'fullness of life'. "I have come that you may have life to the full" (Jn 10:10). The promise is for now, and for eternity. Who could in their right mind decline such an invitation! Yet people do turn away all the time. We are not to be deterred by this apathy or hostility. Our task is to go further to the most unlikely people who may be more open and ready to respond. The banquet hall must be full.

We offer the greatest treasure

What we have to offer is not some temporary 'fix' for the distressed, nor some technique to be more successful, nor some panacea from the pain of modern living. It is more than this. We offer the saving love of God which awakens the heart to lasting joy, not just some temporary relief from the pressures of daily existence. We offer eternal life to be found through faith in Christ. We offer a sure guarantee of the lasting experience of resurrection hope. We know that those who find Christ, or rather allow Christ to find them, have "a sure hope, and the promise of an inheritance that can never be spoilt or soiled and never fade way" (1 Pet 1:3-4). No matter what the trials and tribulations they have in life, they will be grounded in a joy that can never be taken away from them. They are "sure of the end to which their faith looks forward, that is, the salvation of their souls" (1 Pet 1:9).

How should we meet our contemporaries with this good news? How can we convince them? Only by the grace of God will hearts change and real conversion occur. Yet the way we share the good news is critical. First, we must ourselves be deeply convinced of the truth of Jesus, the reality of eternal life, and the urgency of the salvation message. Second, we must love as Jesus has loved, with no implied condemnation or superior attitude. We must avoid any paternalistic attitude or implication that we stand on higher ground. Rather we are but beggars showing other beggars where to find the bread of life. We are but broken sinners who by the grace of God have found the incredible sweetness of salvation, and want to share this with others. Third, our lives must speak the truth before our mouths utter anything. We need to be living the gospel radically according to what is appropriate for our state of life. Our contemporaries highly value authenticity. Fourth, we must be genuinely joyful in our disposition. The joy of the Lord is hugely attractive. People today are intrigued by joy since there is so little of it in modern living. In an entertainment culture people are trying to find happiness through amusement. In a pleasure seeking culture people pursue all sorts of expensive diversions and holidays to give them a lift in life. But all of this still leaves them shallow and without lasting joy. Inviting people to encounter Jesus through the power of the Holy Spirit is the way to joy. If they have seen the joy in us they will be drawn to Christ and eager to have this new life for themselves.

Fifth, we need to have a vibrant, loving and welcoming community for them to enter without any obligations imposed, but simply because they find refuge, welcome, acceptance and healing in our midst. Sixth, we will need to help them be in a place where they hear the good news proclaimed in the Spirit and are free to make a personal response through repentance and faith. "Faith comes from hearing" not from some form of cultural osmosis. Seventh, we must be prepared to pay the price of accompanying the individual for a relatively long period of time, to be with them in their ups and downs, to listen to their struggles, and to encourage them at all times. Eighth, we need to instruct them on the disciplines of Christian life which will enable them to grow in the Spirit according to the plan of God for their lives. Ninth, we must help them discover the wonder of the sacraments, especially the Eucharist, and how we are sustained by the bread of life. Tenth, we must encourage them to share with others the joy in the Lord they are experiencing. It's never too early to share what God is doing in their lives, since faith grows when it is given away to others.

People coming from death to life

In contemporary post-Christian culture good people are often the 'walking dead', their souls not alive to the Spirit. Deep inside themselves there is an emptiness which they find hard to identify, a nostalgia for the presence of God. Written into every human person is a deep longing for eternal life. We are made for union with God. Our lives misfire without God, even when we attain worldly success and numerous accolades. There is something missing, and in moments of grace people get in touch with this loss. We don't have to try to scare them with the threat of hell. Rather we awaken in them this deep-seated desire for God. Heaven is very attractive, not as some perceived paradise in another world, but as the love of God experienced in the heart, the beginnings of heaven through the Holy Spirit's indwelling presence.

This breakthrough of grace happens in numerous and diverse ways. Some will testify it was in the middle of a dark moment of loneliness and despair, when as an ultimate test they cried out to God. And he came! Light in the darkness, and the darkness could not overcome it. Others share how they arrived at a Christian weekend, dragged along by a persistent friend. There they encountered a tangible love which overwhelmed them, and set them free from bondage to sin, bringing healing to their broken heart, and assurance that Christ is real; not a figment of imagination, but the Risen Saviour who brings lasting hope. Others gradually become intrigued by their Christian friends, the way they negotiate their problems in life, the way they handle family disputes, the way they mourn with hope during bereavement, the way they seem to really care about others, especially those on the fringes of the society. Drawn into connection with the Christian community these friends find themselves changing, at first imperceptibly, but then more consciously, as they sense their heart is melting under the influence of love, and they begin to actively seek God, and open their heart to his loving presence. Repenting, turning away from sin, and turning with faith to the Lord of life, they find the infilling of the Holy Spirit and the hole in the heart begins to be filled. All is new! "For those who are in Christ Jesus there is a new creation; the old is gone and the new is here" (2 Cor 5:17).

The need for a new fire

A major hindrance to the salvation of the world is the apathy in Christian hearts, the over-familiarity with the things of God, the loss of awe and wonder at the beauty and majesty of the risen Christ, a boredom and inertia in the soul, having lost one's 'first love', and doing religion as the grind of duty without joy and without zeal for the Father's house. Paul urges Timothy to "fan into a flame the gift God gave you when hands were laid upon you". This gift God bestowed, Paul reminds his disciple, "was not a spirit of timidity, but the Spirit of power, and love and self-control" (2 Tim 1:6-7). If this fire within us is stoked again and begins to burn furiously we will be ready to "bear the hardships for the sake of the good news, relying on the power of God who has saved us and called us to be holy" (2 Tim 1:8). Paul is encouraging Timothy not to lose what has already been given. Too easily we can succumb to the inertial forces within the soul which deaden our spirit and render us useless for the kingdom of God. The problem is not blatant sinful habits arising again, but the loss of zeal for God and his kingdom. We allow worldly thinking to denude us of our clothing in Christ. Paul urges the Romans, "Do not model yourselves on the behaviour of the world around you, but let your behaviour change, modelled by your new mind" (Rom 12:2). He identifies a real danger! We settle down to a compromise with worldly thinking, no longer sharp in our awareness of the in- breaking kingdom of God. We pray every day "thy kingdom come", but we do not mean it. Habit of religion dominates us, rendering us useless for the kingdom of God. Satan delights in this stance. Nothing could be more damaging to the work of God than a half-hearted Christian, nothing could make the Church more ineffective than an adherent who has become lukewarm and mediocre in living the way of discipleship. Lord, save us from ourselves!

A new wave of the Spirit

Now is the time when God would want to bring a new wave of his Holy Spirit, waking us from our slumber, galvanizing us into action for the Kingdom, stirring our souls to greatness, not by worldly achievements, but through proclaiming the good news to the lost. We will once again say within ourselves, "Zeal for your house, Lord, consumes me" (Jn 2:17). We will allow ourselves to be refined and purified like gold and silver in the furnace. We will hear again the call given to the prophet, "Whom shall I send?" and we will reply wholeheartedly, "Here I am, Lord, send me" (Is 6:8). O Lord, for the kiss of your Spirit upon the Catholic Church today! That the sleeping giant may wake up and go forward to proclaim your love.

In this present age we have a privileged moment of the Holy Spirit, an unparalleled outpouring of the Spirit across the globe. At the same time, we have a new generation who have not experienced even the remnants of Christendom, fragmented as it is in today's culture. They are more ready than ever to receive the good news. They are honest, more authentic about their deepest needs. They articulate a spiritual hunger, but do not know where to fulfill this hunger. Totally experimental, they will try anything. Let's be there to guide them to Christ, the only lasting answer to the deepest questions of the heart, the only ultimate fulfillment for the human soul.

We don't fall into the 'fulfillment gospel', as if all that Christ offers is self-satisfaction. We offer them fullness of life through repentance and self-denial, through embracing the cross as their salvation and as the way to find life by dying to self. The good news is soothing to the soul since it firstly brings us the overwhelming love of God revealed in Jesus. But then our response becomes one of genuine conversion, breaking with the old way of life and taking on the new. Those who have been won by the love of God do this readily without much coaxing at all because the soul has new eyes to see and a new compass by which to find the genuine direction to wholeness; not by self-fulfillment but by being filled with God.

While Arthur Stace made his heroic response over a lifetime chalking the word "Eternity" on the pavements of Sydney, maybe we will seek alternative creative ways to reach our contemporaries. The message of eternity will surely be at the centre of our proclamation. We may ask the question of ourselves: "Have I been lulled into complacency due to my unwitting alliance with the culture of our day, joining the mind-set of the 'walking dead', who would do anything to forget real death?" That way of thinking deadens the soul. We must "get real". This fleeting sojourn on planet earth has no real meaning if we deny eternity. After all, eternity in heaven is simply God. He is our destiny. And it begins now. Yet when we cross over the threshold of death we no longer are in time as we know it, that is, chronos time which we can measure by seconds, minutes, hours, days and years. In heaven we enter into the eternal now! A mind-blowing concept! God will be all in all.

It is good to long for heaven, but not to escape into the clouds. It is good to proclaim eternity, but not to encourage people to opt out of the call to love others and to work for justice now. Our over-riding desire for God should give us a motive for living well now, a meaning and purpose that transcends this earthly state, but challenges us to work to build a more loving and just society now. We are but pilgrims here, knowing that our ultimate homeland is beyond this world as we know it. If we are motivated by love of God, our pilgrim journey will leave a legacy of practical love. Many lives, especially those of the poor and abandoned, will be enriched through the selfless work we have done. Yet, we will not be trapped in a one-dimensional existence. Rather, we will always trust that, ultimately, we will be caught up in the glory of God, sharing in the beauty of all things made new, and in communion with all the saints, enjoying the love of God forever.

ENDNOTES

[1] Fr Ken Barker, *Amazing Love*, Connor Court Publishing

[2] This story is taken from Roy Williams with Elizabeth Meyers, Mr Eternity: the story of Arthur Stace, (Sydney: Acorn Press, 2017).

[3] Ibid., 43

[4] Ibid., 85

[5] Ibid., 100

[6] Ibid., 112

[7] Ibid., 113

[8] Ibid., 198

[9] Ibid., 207

[10] St Augustine, *Confessions*

[11] Johannes Hartl, *Heart Fire* (Edinburgh: Muddy Pearl, 2018) 102-13

[12] *Catechism of the Catholic Church* (*CCC*) 1009

[13] Pope Francis, General Audience, Wednesday 18 October 2017.

[14] Pope Francis, General Audience, Wednesday 11 October 2017

[15] Pope Francis, General Audience, Wednesday 25 October 2017

[16] St Faustina Kowalska, *Diary*, 1146

[17] Pope Francis, General Audience, Wednesday 25 October 2017

[18] St Thérèse of Lisieux, *The Collected Letters*, trans. F.J. Sheed (London: Sheed and Ward, 1949) (*LT*) 63

[19] St Thérèse of Lisieux, *LT*, 74

[20] Ibid, *LT*, 225

[21] See Conrad de Mester, *With Empty Hands: the message of Thérèse of Lisieux* (Homebush: St Paul Publications, 1982).

[22] Athanasius, *On the Incarnation*, 58

[23] Ignatius of Antioch, Letter to the Romans, 4, in *Early Christian Writings*, (N.Y.: Penguin books, 1968) 104

[24] Ibid., 7, 106

[25] Athanasius, *On the Incarnation*, 57

[26] Martyrdom of the Holy Martyrs of Carthage, 18-21

[27] The story taken from Boniface Hanley OFM, Maximilian Kolbe, in *Ten Christians* (Notre Dame: Ave Maria Press, 1979) 93-117

[28] Boniface Hanley OFM, *Maximilian Kolbe: No Greater Love* (Ave Maria Press, 1982) 72

[29] Pope John Paul II, *Dives in Misericordia*, 13

[30] St Faustina Kowalska, *Diary, Divine Mercy in My Soul*, No. 301

[31] Congregation for the Doctrine of the Faith, *Letter on Certain Questions of Eschatology*, 17 May 1979

[32] Pope Francis, General Audience, 11 December 2013

[33] Pope Francis, Angelus, St Peters Square, 26 November 2017

[34] Walter Kasper, *Mercy* (N.Y.: Paulist Press, 2013) 102

[35] Nicholas Diat, *A Time to Die: Monks on the threshold of eternal life* (San Francisco, Ignatius Press, 2018) 19-31

[36] Pope Paul VI, *Credo of the People of God*, 30

[37] https://catholicleader.com.au/uncategorized/former-atheist-and-political-leader-bill-hayden-baptised-at-age-85-at-st-marys-church-ipswich

[38] Pope John Paul II, General Audience, Wednesday 4 August 1999

[39] Vatican II, *Lumen Gentium*, 49

[40] St Thérèse of Lisieux, *The Final Conversations*, trans John Clarke (Washington DC: ICS, 1977) 102

[41] Patrick Ahern, *Maurice and Thérèse: The Story of a Love* (NY: Doubleday, 1998) 161

[42] Ibid., 166

[43] Ibid., 167

[44] USA Today.com/story/tech/nation-now 2018/03/14 heaven-fairy-story.

[45] *CCC*, 1024

[46] Raniero Cantalamessa, *Life in the Lordship of Christ*, 84

[47] Brennan Manning, *The Furious Longing of God* (Colorado Springs: David Cook, 2009) 53-55. While Brennan Manning failed to represent the whole gospel at times he presented this aspect of the message well.

[48] Jennifer Moorcroft, *He is My Heaven: The Life of Elizabeth of the Trinity* (Washington DC: ICS Publications, 2001) 84

⁴⁹ Pope Francis, General Audience, Paul VI Audience Hall, Wednesday, 2 February 2022

⁵⁰ Pope John Paul II, *Redemptoris Mater*, 38-41

⁵¹ St John of the Cross, *The Living Flame of Love*, Stanza 1, in *The Collected Works of St John of the Cross*, tr Kieran Kavanaugh, OCD and Otilio Rodriguez, OCD (Washington, DC: ICS Publications, 1973) 578

⁵² Ibid., 335

⁵³ Joseph Ratzinger, *Eschatology: Death and Eternal Life* (Washington, DC: The Catholic University of America Press, 1988) 229

⁵⁴ Ibid., 230

⁵⁵ Ibid., 231

⁵⁶ Piet Fransen, "The doctrine of Purgatory" in *Eastern Churches Quarterly*, No. 13, 1959, 106

⁵⁷ Frederick M. Jones, *Alphonsus de Liguori* (Dublin: Gill and McMillan, 1992) 258

⁵⁸ *CCC*, 1033

⁵⁹ Vatican II, *Lumen Gentium*, 48

⁶⁰ St Faustina Kowalska, *Diary*, 741

⁶¹ Pope Francis, Morning Meditation in Chapel of the Domus Sanctae Marthae, Tuesday, 22 November 2016

⁶² *CCC*, 1035

⁶³ Dante, *Inferno*, Canto XXXIV

⁶⁴ Pope Francis, Prayer Vigil for the 19th Memorial and Commitment Day, sponsored by the Libera Foundation of Fr Luigi Ciotti, Church of San Gregorio VII, Rome, Friday, 21 March 2014

⁶⁵ C.S. Lewis, *The Great Divorce*, in the Complete Signature Classics (San Francisco: Harper, 2002) 327

⁶⁶ Ibid., 339

⁶⁷ Bernard of Clairveaux, *De Grad. Hum.*, X, 36

⁶⁸ Hans Urs Von Balthasar, Dare We Hope That All Men Be Saved?, San Francisco: Ignatius Press, 1988

⁶⁹ Mary Ann Fatula, *Catherine of Siena's Way* (Collegeville: Liturgical Press, 1987), 202-203

[70] Avery Dulles, "The Population of Hell", *First Things*, 133, May 2003, 37

[71] Vatican II, *Lumen Gentium*, 14

[72] A thorough exposition of the meaning of Vatican II's doctrine on salvation can be found in Ralph Martin, *Will Many be Saved?* (Michigan: Wm. B. Eerdmans Publishing Co., 2012)

[73] For an elaboration of this issue, see Fr Ken Barker, *Amazing Love* (Ballan: Connor Court, 2012), 67-71

[74] See Ralph Martin, op. cit. This book and the follow-up entitled *A Church in Crisis* (Steubenville: Emmaus publishing, 2020) offer a prophetic call for the Church to clarify its thinking on salvation and avoid a universalistic approach. The theme of these books suggests a grim outlook on the Church and its contemporary mission, suggesting even Pope Francis has gone astray. This author would not agree with that suggestion.

[75] St Thomas Aquinas, *Summa Theologica*, Supplement to Part III, Quest. 94, Art. 2, 3

[76] *CCC*, 997

[77] Lateran Council IV (1215) DS801

[78] For Aquinas' treatment of the resurrected body see *Summa Theologiae* III supp., 75-85

[79] Maurice Carrez, "With what body do the dead rise again?" in *Concilium*, Vol. 60 (NY: Herder and Herder, 1970) 103-114

[80] For longer discussion see George Maloney, *The Everlasting Now* (Notre Dame: Ave Maria Press, 1979) 182-185

[81] Ignatius of Antioch, *Letter to the Ephesians*, 20.2

[82] Joseph Ratzinger, Called to Communion: Understanding the Church Today, trans. Adrian Walker (San Francisco: Ignatius Press, 1996), 37

[83] *CCC*, 1524

[84] *CCC*, 675

[85] A well-known popular website is *Countdown to the Kingdom*, hosted by Catholic authors. The site promotes unapproved and highly questionable seers, such as Fr Michael Rodriguez from Canada and Edson Glauber, a Brazilian. A critique is offered by Emmett O'Regan, *Apocalypse When? Catholic Millenarianism Rising?* 7 September 2020

[86] Insight given by Antonio Spadaro SJ, *Defy the Apocalypse*, La Civilta Cattolica,

20 January 2020

[87] *CCC*, 676

[88] See Peter S. Williamson, *Revelation* (Grand Rapids, Michigan: Baker Publishing, 2015). This book gives a balanced presentation, showing that the author is focused on the "already" attained victory proclaimed to comfort those under persecution, and also the promise of the Parousia which is yet to arrive. The centre of the proclamation is the victory in Christ, who is destined to be all in all.

[89] *CCC*, 1039

[90] *CCC*, 1042

[91] Vatican II, *Lumen Gentium*, 48

[92] Ibid., 1

[93] *CCC*, 1045

[94] Irenaeus, *Adversus Haereses*, 5:32

[95] Ibid., 5:36, 1

[96] Vatican II, *Gaudium et Spes*, 39

APPENDIX

INDULGENCES (CCC 1472- 1479)

The Catechism defines an indulgence as a "remission before God of the temporal punishment due to sins whose guilt has already been forgiven". We need to explain this carefully.

Temporal punishment due to sin

While the language is unfortunately foreign to the contemporary mind, we need to grasp what temporal punishment due to sin means. The consequence of grave sin, which deprives us of union with God, is *eternal* punishment. Any other lesser sin, because it causes disorder in our relationship with God, carries with it temporal punishment.

The language of punishment is problematic to the contemporary mind since, as the Catechism warns, it could lead us to see God as arbitrarily ready to inflict punishment on us whenever we put a foot out of order. Rather, we are meant to understand that the "punishment" does not derive from God's attitude, but simply because of our own sinful actions by which we condemn ourselves.

After we have been forgiven mortal sin, we still have remaining temporal punishment due to the sin committed. While forgiveness is given by God without reserve, the offender still needs to make up for the disorder the sin has caused. An easy way to understand this is in the case of stealing. A person can be fully forgiven, but still needs to repair the damage done by returning the stolen goods, or doing some penance in reparation.

The purifying fire of purgatory lifts from us all temporal punishment due to forgiven mortal sins and also any unforgiven venial sins and their effects.

Granting Indulgences

The Church has a long-standing practice of mercifully granting indulgences. An indulgence is a remission before God of the temporal punishment due to sins when the guilt has been forgiven. The Lord has given the Church the power to forgive sins through the Sacrament of Reconciliation. The priest will give a penance for the penitent to do as part of their reparation. This power is extended outside of the sacrament when the Church grants an indulgence. In granting an indulgence the Church prescribes certain conditions to be fulfilled. For example, that a prayer be said for the intentions of the Holy Father, and an Our Father, Hail Mary, and Glory be is said. Sometimes particular conditions are attached to the indulgence, such as praying at a designated shrine, or fulfilling conditions for a pilgrimage etc.

We can gain an indulgence either for ourselves or for a soul in purgatory. It can be partial or plenary depending on whether it removes part or all of the temporal punishment due to sin.

As members of the communion of saints wanting to help those of our beloved who have died, we not only have Masses celebrated for the repose of their souls but we also seek to gain indulgences for them. This practice is an expression of the teaching on the communion of saints which I addressed earlier; that the pilgrim church on earth, the suffering church in purgatory and the triumphant church in heaven are deeply connected and interrelated in Christ, and seek to help one another.

www.ingramcontent.com/pod-product-compliance
Lightning Source LLC
Chambersburg PA
CBHW061604110426
42742CB00039B/2790